JAMES JONES

H B J   A L B U M   B I O G R A P H I E S
edited by Matthew J. Bruccoli

ROSS MACDONALD by Matthew J. Bruccoli
JACK KEROUAC by Tom Clark
JAMES JONES by George Garrett

JAMES JONES
by GEORGE GARRETT

HARCOURT BRACE JOVANOVICH, PUBLISHERS
San Diego   New York   London

Requests for permission to make copies of any part
of the work should be mailed to:
Permissions, Harcourt Brace Jovanovich, Publishers,
Orlando, Florida 32887

The publisher and author thank the following institutions for
permission to reprint materials from the James Jones Papers:
Collection of American Literature, the Beinecke Rare Book and
Manuscript Library, Yale University; Humanities Research Center,
The University of Texas at Austin; Charles Scribner's Sons and
The Library, Princeton University, for Charles Scribner's Sons
Archives at Princeton University. Grateful acknowledgment is also
made to Gloria Jones, Shelby Foote, David R. Slavitt, David Ray,
and Jim Hall for their generous cooperation in granting permission
to reprint excerpts from their letters and other unpublished materials.
All photographs not otherwise credited are courtesy of Gloria Jones.

Library of Congress Cataloging in Publication Data
Garrett, George P., 1929–
James Jones.
Bibliography: p.
Includes index.
1. Jones, James, 1921–1977. 2. Novelists, American—
20th century—Biography. I. Title.
PS3560.049Z66   1984   813'.54 [B]   83-18665
ISBN 0-15-146049-3
ISBN 0-15-645955-8 (pbk.)

Designed by Joy Chu
Printed in the United States of America
First edition
A B C D E

HBJ

FOR GLORIA JONES
AND FOR SUSAN GARRETT,
both of whom, separately and equally,
have kept the faith

I would like to leave books behind me to let people know that I have lived. I'd like to think that people would read them avidly, as I have read so many and would feel the sadness and frustration and joy and love I tried to put in them, that people would think about that guy James Jones and wish they had known the guy who could write like that.

James Jones[1]

What Jones wins on is his utter dedication to the truth—truth at all costs, and no matter what it does to any other factor in the novel. Even the roughness of his writing, the awkwardness and innocence of ideas in almost any form, gives strength to this aspect of almost everything he wrote.

Shelby Foote[2]

CONTENTS

· · ·

Contents

PREFACE

Most novelists are too vain to write
biographies of other novelists, particularly
contemporaries. I wouldn't want to write
their biographies.

James Jones[3]

·   ·   ·

O N E could not begin to write a biography of James Jones, even a brief
one such as this is, without gratefully building on the good labors of those
who have gone before. I have listed and acknowledged many articles, reviews, newspaper pieces, and interviews within the text and in the bibliography. I owe much to all of them. And all of us are indebted to John R.
Hopkins for *James Jones: A Checklist* (1974) which contains so much
accurate and useful information and, as well, an important interview with
Jones. In addition to extensive critical materials, James R. Giles's *James
Jones* (1981) offers a good deal of solidly factual biographical detail, compiled with the generous assistance of Gloria Jones. Willie Morris' *James
Jones: A Friendship* (1978) is at once biography and memoir, a literary
appreciation and a celebration of an artist. Again, thanks to the aid and
comfort of Mrs. Jones, this account is richly threaded with significant
biographical material. It is especially fine and detailed in its treatment of
the Paris years and of the final years at Sagaponack. Above all Willie

Morris defines and demonstrates a great deal of the character of James Jones, honoring his courage, his discipline, his humor, his charm, his generosity, his huge vitality, and his impeccable integrity. Every other piece of evidence I have examined, from letters to and from Jones to the most private jottings in journals, supports the sense of character which Morris presents.

Frank MacShane, already enviably recognized as a distinguished biographer, is hard at work on a large scale, authorized biography of James Jones, one which promises to go much deeper and well beyond all of these others, including my own. Inevitably there are questions which only he will be able to answer, details which only he will be able to make clear for us. Meanwhile I am most deeply grateful to him and to Gloria Jones for kind permission, indeed encouragement, to use many of the available materials as best I could. I have done so with the full confidence that any errors which appear here, despite all my best intentions, will be corrected in due time.

Above all, any biographer of James Jones owes (as do we all) an incalculable debt to Jones himself. There are the many interviews of him, his magazine articles, his two nonfiction books, personal comments about himself and his work—as, for example, in the brief introductions to the stories in *The Ice-Cream Headache and Other Stories*—and his conscientious and candid replies to queries for reference, texts (especially important is his statement in *Twentieth Century Authors*, edited by Stanley Kunitz). There are characteristics throughout all these materials which make them more useful than they might be in the cases of many other writers. One is an amazing consistency. Allowing for growing and changing, maturing in experience and wisdom over time, there nevertheless remains a deep consistency in his views on life and art. And the most constant quality of that consistency is his unquenchable integrity. That same integrity seems to have been crucial to his character from the beginning; for the *facts* of his life, as he reveals and describes them, early and late, do not change. Not even in emphasis. I have caught him, here and there and very rarely, in minor exaggerations, slight and graceful distortions of fact. But never once in a lie. He did not—*could* not, it seems—even edge toward lying in his public self. He learned soon enough that publicity is an essential ingredient of contemporary salesmanship; and having been burned a number of times early on in his career, he was careful and controlled, guarded with newsmen, critics, reviewers, and the like. Yet he never backed away from principles. His private notes and his letters, letters now preserved by the hundreds in Yale's Beinecke Library, by the thousands at Texas' Humanities Research Center, and in the Scribner's Archives at Princeton University, support the public facts of his life and uniformly demonstrate the same rigorous and admirable integrity. I can find no instance where he ever cheated or sought to deceive anyone. Recently John Aldridge told me of the time, in the spring of 1959, when he and Jones had been together at a critical seminar in Blérancourt in France. He especially remarked on Jones's "sincerity and wonderful simplicity." Do you think any of that was a scam? I had to ask. "Well . . . if it was, it was a damn good one."[4]

More than any other writer I have known or known of, writers of our times, James Jones was, and therefore is, a man to be trusted. He can even be trusted to admit the plain truth: that, at a certain point, after the experience of writing about characters closely modeled on himself and on others, so that the experience of creating has now become part of memory also, he can no longer honestly remember what "really" happened and what didn't. He can only truly remember what has been wedded together in the fiction. As he wrote in "Hawaiian Recall," that wonderful epilogue to *Viet Journal*: "I remembered the times I had watched Air Force pilot officers drunk and fighting on the Royal Hawaiian's lawn after Midway— or was that Prewitt?" And again in the same piece:

> I had once marched up to Kole Kole alone—twice, two times—with a full field pack and an escorting noncom, over some stupid argument with my company commander. I had used the incident on Prewitt in the novel, and it had been reproduced in the film version. Now I no longer knew whether Prewitt had done it, or I had.[5]

So the other accounts of James Jones's life, those in print and those derived from interviews with people who knew him, found in his own words in his literary works, in his letters and notebooks, on the backs of envelopes, menus, and any other handy pieces of paper, have made this accounting of mine more pleasure than labor, more a privilege than a chore. It has been an honor to know him.

·   ·   ·

THERE are sources for all the facts presented here. All the inferences, interpretation, and speculation are more or less my own. Nobody else should be blamed for them.

MANY people were very helpful to me in putting this book together. I am grateful to them all. I owe a special debt to Richard M. Ludwig of the Princeton University Library, to David Schoonover of the Beinecke Library, and to Decherd Turner, Ellen Dunlap, and Cathy Henderson of the Humanities Research Center, University of Texas. I also have special gratitude and obligations toward Harry Antrim, Ruthe Battestin, Madison Bell, John Ciardi, R. H. W. Dillard, Richard Elman, Shelby Foote, Jim and Debby Hall, Robert Hodesh, David Ray, David Slavitt, Pat Srebrnik, Charleen Swansea, Jo Ann Thompson and the Robinson Chamber of Commerce, Chapin Vasilake, and Jon Manchip White. I also extend my thanks to the Robinson Township Library and to the libraries of Hollins College, University of Michigan, University of Virginia, Virginia Military Institute, and Washington and Lee University.

G. G.

CHRONOLOGY

•   •   •

November 6, 1921	Birth of James Ramon Jones to Ramon Jones and Ada Blessing Jones, Robinson, Illinois.
November 10, 1939	Enlists in U.S. Army (Serial No. 6915544) at Chanute Field, Illinois. Sent first to Fort Slocum, New York (Barracks 85-s) ; then, by troopship and via Puerto Rico and the Panama Canal to Hawaii; stationed there in Army Air Corps at Hickham Field and Wheeler Field.
March 2, 1941	Death of Ada Blessing Jones.
July 25, 1941	Transferred from Air Corps to Infantry; now in 27th Infantry Regiment at Schofield Barracks.
December 7, 1941	Japanese attack Pearl Harbor; Jones on guard duty as runner at D Quad, Schofield Barracks.
March 11, 1942	His father commits suicide in Robinson.

June 1942– October 1942	Attends University of Hawaii part-time, taking Creative Writing and English Masterpieces on Monday, Wednesday, and Friday for five credit hours.
October 19, 1942	25th Infantry Division alerted for action.
December 6, 1942	Ships out for Guadalcanal, sailing at 1:00 P.M. (1300 hours).
January 1, 1943	Lands at Guadalcanal.
January 11–13, 1943	His outfit, F Company of 27th Infantry Regiment, goes into combat. Jones is wounded on 12 January.
May 1943	Arriving from New Zealand on hospital ship *Matsonia*, Jones is sent first to Letterman General Hospital in San Francisco, then shipped to Kennedy General Hospital at Memphis, Tennessee.
June 1943– June 1944	Kennedy General Hospital; then 842nd QM Gas Supply Company; then K Company, 101st Infantry, 26th Infantry Division, Camp Campbell, Kentucky; on 5 June 1944, a patient in the Station Hospital, Camp Campbell.
November 3, 1943	Meets Lowney Handy.
July 6, 1944	Honorably discharged from Army at Camp Campbell, Kentucky. Returns to Robinson to live with Mr. and Mrs. Harry E. Handy, at 202 W. Mulberry Street, and to write.
January– June 1945	Lives in New York City. Meets Maxwell Perkins. Attends New York University under Veterans Vocational Rehabilitation Program.
July–August 1945	Living and writing in Maggie, North Carolina. Returns to Illinois.
January 22, 1946	Scribner's receives completed manuscript of his novel "They Shall Inherit the Laughter."
February 16, 1946	Telegram from Maxwell Perkins rejects "Laughter," but offers $500 option for "Stewart novel" (*From Here to Eternity*).
February 17, 1946	Jones accepts offer.
June 27, 1946	Graduates from Red Cross First Aid, Water Safety, and Accident Prevention School at Pine Mountain State Park, Chipley, Georgia.

July 30, 1946	Option on *From Here to Eternity* is renewed.
June 18, 1947	Death of Maxwell Perkins.
July 9, 1947	Burroughs Mitchell becomes his editor at Scribner's.
December 4, 1947	Option for *From Here to Eternity* is renewed.
January 19, 1948	Edward Weeks, editor of *Atlantic*, accepts Jones's short story "Temper of Steel." His first published work.
February 27, 1950	Completes first draft of *From Here to Eternity*.
April 21, 1950	Scribner's contract for *From Here to Eternity*.
September 18, 1950	Receives advance of $2,000 on next novel—*Some Came Running*.
September 20, 1950	Galley proof of *From Here to Eternity* mailed to Jones in Marshall, Illinois—First Class Special Delivery from Grand Central Post Office at 9:00 P.M. Received in Marshall at 11:00 A.M. on 22 September.
December 16, 1950	*Publishers Weekly* appears with picture of Jones on cover and large advertisement for *From Here to Eternity*.
February 26, 1951	*From Here to Eternity* is published.
March 16, 1951	Contract with Columbia Pictures for film version of *From Here to Eternity*.
1951–1957	Lives mainly in Marshall, Illinois, and in Florida. Builds and furnishes house in Marshall (1 Beech Street Lane). With Harry and Lowney Handy he founds, helps to finance and manage the Handy Colony for writers. Throughout this period he is writing *Some Came Running*.
January 29, 1952	National Book Award for *From Here to Eternity* presented to Jones at Hotel Commodore, New York.
June 5, 1952	Death of Jones's younger sister, Mary Ann (Tink) Jones.
January 18, 1957	Offer of contract for movie rights for *Some Came Running*—$250,000 with no escalator clauses.
February 27, 1957	Married to Gloria Patricia Mosolino in Haiti.
September 1957	Moves to 137 East 67th Street, New York. Writes *The Pistol*.

January 10, 1958	*Some Came Running* is published.
April 12, 1958	Sails for Europe with Gloria on the *Liberté*.
April 19– August 18, 1958	Lives in London, first at Stafford Hotel, then at 61 Eaton Place. Begins *The Thin Red Line*.
August 18, 1958	Arrives in Paris; lives first at 17, Quai Aux Fleurs; later (1960) buys and refurbishes apartment at 10, Quai d'Orléans, Île St.-Louis; Paris will remain Jones's permanent residence until 1974.
January 12, 1959	*The Pistol* is published.
February 1960	Buys apartment in Paris.
August 5, 1960	Kaylie Jones born.
October 19, 1960	Sells house in Marshall, Illinois, for $42,000.
June–October 1961	Paid consultant and writer for Darryl Zanuck's war film *The Longest Day*.
November 1, 1961	Jones returns to United States to finish final revisions of *The Thin Red Line*.
Thanksgiving 1961	Finishes *The Thin Red Line* at home of William Styron in Roxbury, Connecticut.
September 17, 1962	*The Thin Red Line* is published.
Christmas 1962 and New Year's 1963	Vacations in Jamaica. Begins "underwater novel" (*Go to the Widow-Maker*).
November 19, 1964	Writes Burroughs Mitchell and breaks with Scribner's.
December 21, 1964	Receives six-figure, multiple-book contract (with escalator clauses) from Dell Books.
June 30, 1966	Finishes *Go to the Widow-Maker*.
April 10, 1967	*Go to the Widow-Maker* is published.
March 27, 1968	*The Ice-Cream Headache and Other Stories* is published.
February 15, 1971	*The Merry Month of May* is published.
July 27, 1972	Finishes *A Touch of Danger*.
February 26– March 28, 1973	Trip to South Vietnam on assignment for *New York Times Magazine*.
May 11, 1973	*A Touch of Danger* is published.
October 13, 1973	Finishes *Viet Journal*.
January 2, 1974	Accepts offer to teach at Florida International University (Miami).

March 13, 1974	*Viet Journal* is published.
July 5, 1974	Leaves Paris for America, to live.
September 6, 1974– June 13, 1975	Visiting Professor and Writer in Residence at Florida International University. Lives at 251 Island Drive, Key Biscayne.
Summer 1975	Buys house ("Chateau Spud") in Sagaponack, Long Island. Moves there.
September 10, 1975	*WW II* published.
November 17, 1975	Sells Paris apartment for $449,000.
January 14, 1977	Hospitalized for "congestive heart failure as a result of bronchitis" at Southampton (L.I.) Hospital.
March 31, 1977	George W. Jones (Jeff) dies in Roanoke, Virginia.
May 9, 1977	James Jones dies at 7:50 P.M.
May 15, 1977	Memorial service for Jones held at Bridgehampton Community House.
February 22, 1978	*Whistle* published. Publication party at East Side Armory in New York.

Writing has to keep evolving into deeper honesty, like everything else, and you cannot stand on past precident [sic] or theory, and still evolve. You remember that.

James Jones[1]

PART ONE
• • • •
A REAPPRAISAL

· · ·

FOLLOWING the death of James Jones in May of 1977, there were three successive waves of public reaction. The first, at the time of his death, brought obituaries and encomiums, various published eulogies and recollections. Next, in 1978, came the publication of *Whistle*, the third and final novel of his World War II trilogy which began with *From Here to Eternity* and included *The Thin Red Line*. Jones had almost completed the long, hard work on *Whistle* at the time of his death. In fact, using a tape recorder given to him by Joseph Heller, he continued to work on the last part of the story even as his life was fading in the intensive care unit of Southampton Hospital. The posthumous publication of *Whistle*, its final pages put together from Jones's notes and according to his wishes by his friend Willie Morris, inevitably evoked a great deal of serious critical attention. There was much discussion in the reviews not only of the place of *Whistle* in Jones's trilogy and his lifework as a whole, but also of Jones's place in the literary history of this nation and these times. Then *Whistle* was followed, within that same year, by Willie Morris's *James Jones: A Friendship*, bringing forth the third round of reviews and reconsiderations, this time from a somewhat different point of view; for the critics also had to consider the validity of Morris' picture of Jones.

By the end of 1978, then, a kind of general critical consensus had emerged. Basically this view was that Jones had earned for himself an enduring place in the history of American literature, chiefly as the author of the trilogy of war novels. Thus, in 1981, when James R. Giles published the first book-length treatment and assessment of Jones's work, he felt safe, almost beyond question or possible challenge, in asserting in his Preface: "This three-volume work is our most important fictional treatment of U.S. involvement in World War II."[2] Taken together with *The Pistol* and some of the short stories and articles, and especially with the well-received and highly personal text Jones created for *WWII*, his work could legitimately be classified as the foremost American accounting of World War II. Which is no minor place, no small achievement, when you consider the number and variety of novels and of nonfiction works that have been concerned with aspects of the American experience of that conflict and that are still being produced and published almost forty years after the events.

Among the books of the trilogy, the general critical consensus is that *From Here to Eternity* represents his finest achievement, that this, his first novel dealing with the lost and gone world of the peacetime Regular Army up through and including the Japanese attack on Pearl Harbor, is clearly his best work. During Jones's lifetime, his close friend Budd Schulberg felt no compunction against using the case of *From Here to Eternity* as an example of the masterpiece which was not to be equaled or repeated. In *The Four Seasons of Success* he asked the question, "Why are the odds so high that James Jones will never write another *From Here to Eternity*, that Ralph Ellison will never write another *Invisible Man*, just as Richard Wright never wrote another *Native Son*?"[3] Partly this judgment reflects the enormous commercial and critical success which the novel enjoyed. It became a landmark in the literature of postwar writers in America. It was one of those very rare books that seem to change things, a permanent cultural reference point, something which happened and after which nothing was ever quite the same again. Certainly Jones's life was changed, suddenly and irrevocably in the classic fairy-tale tradition of American success stories. He could look back honestly enough upon himself and his life as it had been before *Eternity* happened, and he never completely ceased to do so; but there was never again any way *to go back to* the life he had known. Indeed, he found it extremely difficult to continue to live his life as he wanted to. He experienced completely what Tennessee Williams, after *The Glass Menagerie*, called "the Catastrophe of Success." It is an old American story almost conventional in its details, yet one which is constantly renewed in each day's headlines. Like so many others to whom this amazing transformation has occurred, Jones had wanted it to happen to him, without, of course, quite knowing what it might mean or how to enjoy and endure it. In a half-ironic, half-wishful way, he seems to have vaguely expected it to happen. While he was still working hard on the manuscript of *From Here to Eternity*, back in 1949, he wrote to his friend and editor at Scribner's, Burroughs Mitchell, a cheerful, confident letter about the book to be: "I want this Pearl Harbor to be good. As good as Tolstoy's Austerlitz, or Stendhal's Waterloo—at least it [*sic*] want it to compare with them. . . . I am fully expecting it to be a best-seller and a Book of the Month Club selection."[4] Which, in fact, it soon was. Yet when he heard that the Book-of-the-Month Club had selected *From Here to Eternity* as an alternate selection, he readily admitted his surprise to Mitchell. "You know," he wrote, "things are happening so thick and fast lately that its [*sic*] getting hard for me to assimilate them."[5] Years later in an interview he described his feelings about the success of *From Here to Eternity* with characteristic candor. "I guess I always believed it would be that kind of success—which is kind of stupid," Jones said. "I just accepted it and took it all for granted. Now I realize of course that it was truly a phenomenon."[6]

Up to and even including the success which came to Jones for *From Here to Eternity*, we are at least, even as Jones was, in more or less familiar territory. Beyond that, though, the story takes another turn. Sudden and overwhelming success did not severely damage him as it did some other very good writers of his same generation. It can be well argued—and has been as, for example, in John Leggett's *Ross and Tom*, which treats the sad lives of Ross Lockridge (*Raintree County*, 1948) and Tom Heggen (*Mister Roberts*, 1946)—that the American version of success can be utterly destructive. "Success itself," Leggett writes, "even when we know it to be fantasy, holds out such promise to us all—fame, money, power and love. They are reasonable promises to the soundest minds, and the compulsion to succeed can become an obsession over which no one has control."[7]

Scribner's bookstore window display for Eternity, *1951*

*Picking up fan mail, Ft. Lauderdale,
1951* (Pete Purinton)

On the beach, Ft. Lauderdale, 1950s

Portrait at the time of Some Came Running,
late 1950s

With William Styron, early 1970s

Somehow Jones survived the experience of having his dreams come true. The truth is Jones was not even especially inhibited by the sudden arrival of fame and fortune. He managed, gracefully and cheerfully enough, to withstand a multitude of large and small pressures and still to keep working and finally to produce his next novel, the enormous and enormously ambitious *Some Came Running*.

And then he was truly tested; for the book was widely and brutally savaged by most of the critics. Jones was personally ridiculed and roughly treated. In years of studying the critical receptions of books, old and new, I have never seen anything quite to match the harsh treatment accorded Jones and *Some Came Running*. Of course, a negative reaction was not wholly unexpected. In 1956, while he was finishing the novel, he wrote Mitchell that "I know everybody is alerted to the end of this one, and know that all the barbs and hooks and knives and harpoons with which literary people love to score each other are being sharpened up no doubt."[8] And somewhat later Burroughs Mitchell, finishing up a letter concerned with necessary cuts and revisions, offered an encouraging conclusion. "I've one thing to add, Jim," he wrote, "now that I've finished *Some Came Running*. That is to say that I think it is a great piece of work; that I think it will last."[9] But there were plenty of problems, not the least of which was the fact that Scribner's itself was divided in its support of the novel. In *The Education of an Editor* (1980) Mitchell recalls that some of his colleagues "disliked" *Some Came Running* "which did not increase my fortitude."[10] In a full-scale piece about Jones and the book, "From Eternity to Here," *Newsweek* predicted a rough time for the book, a book described as "a massive, blunt-nosed hammer stroke at the Middle West which will probably attract a great deal of controversy and very little critical acclaim."[11] This proved to be polite understatement, in terms of the critical fire storm which raged through January and after.

James Jones was not indifferent to the reaction to the results of his labors, and he was fully aware of all that was happening to him. Jones subscribed to press clipping services here (Romeike Press Clippings) and in London (Durrant's Press Clippings). He preserved his wealth of clippings among his papers, and there is every indication that he read them and considered them even when they did not deserve much thoughtful attention. With the appearance of his second book (itself a best-seller, though not on the scale of *Eternity*), he found himself labeled by critics as a one-book writer. With only a few exceptions, they had honored *From Here to Eternity*. Now, with few exceptions, they wrote off *Some Came Running* and, to an extent, the rest of his work—sight unseen. He endured this, unquestionably wounded yet undeniably undeterred.

Within a year he had published *The Pistol*, winning back a few of the same critics who had eagerly, if prematurely, buried him.

Thereafter Jones continued a productive professional writing career for the rest of his life. Throughout his career, however, and even posthumously, he was described by many arbiters of taste and makers and breakers of literary reputations as, at his very best, a *one subject* man; they argued that he could write well and credibly about men at war and, in fact, one war—World War II. And throughout his career he was regularly reminded (just in case he might have suppressed the memory) of the earlier pronouncements that he had never managed to create anything quite as good as *From Here to Eternity*. For these critics to say that, to argue their case with any credibility and persuasion, it was necessary for them to admit *Eternity* into a prominent and permanent place in American letters. Even the most hostile critics, by and large, accorded honor to *From Here to Eternity*. And even some of his honest admirers—for example, Joan Didion in her elegantly moving *Esquire* piece, "Good-bye, Gentleman-ranker"— have tended to avoid hassles, if not the issue, by focusing full attention on that masterpiece and ignoring the rest.[12]

Consider the irony of the man who had wanted to be "a great writer," of whom a piece in *Life* magazine had asserted, "His stated aim in life is the achievement of immortality through his work. . . ."[13] Consider that he was fully conscious of what earning and having a place in American literature might mean and was honestly eager to earn such a place for himself. In a surviving draft of an untitled and unpublished story, written while he was still in the Army, Jones might have been talking directly about himself. "Sergeant David Michael Robertson was a typical peacetime soldier, a thirty year man—with but one exception: he had the faculty of standing off from himself and other people, even as he thought and acted like a typical soldier, and seeing behind the thoughts and actions of himself and his kind. He also had a burning ambition that was as unquenchable as the moon must have been at one time: he wanted to be a great writer."[14] Consider that James Jones was awarded just that—a significant place in the record of American literature—but in compensation, as it were, for the plaudits awarded to his first book, the rest of his life work was treated as inconsequential.

It is to the lasting credit of James Jones that he did not permit any of these things to change him much or to distract him from his labors and certainly not to becloud his good judgment. True, he may have undervalued *The Pistol*, calling it "a sort of equation all studied and planned out in advance." And then adding, "In this sense 'Pistol' is the only book by me written in this way."[15] And he had seen the critical response flip-flop from the negativism which greeted *Some Came Running*. He surely had read Granville Hicks ("The Shorter and Better Jones," *Saturday Review*) in which Hicks concluded that *The Pistol* was "a good book" and used it to ask a serious question. "Does it [*The Pistol*] indicate a change of heart, or did Jones write it just to show that he can be a disciplined writer if he sets out to be?"[16] He seems to have let some of his contempt for the critics rub off on *Pistol*, viewing the book as something easy for critics to like. In "The Writer Speaks: A Conversation between James Jones and Leslie Hanscom," Jones lightly dismisses *The Pistol*, telling his interviewer that *"The Pistol was an attempt at a short symbolic novel, you know, I mean a deliberately symbolic novel, consciously symbolic, which is the way the Europeans write, just a sort of exercise."*[17]

Jones may also have overstressed the virtues of *Some Came Running*, which he often cited, in public and privately, as a particular favorite and perhaps his best work, as if to defend it and, as well, to protect the young, hopeful man who had written his heart into it from the chill blast of derision. In a letter from France to an American woman who had written him an appreciative note about *Some Came Running*, he said: "I still think it is the best single work I have ever written, and certain parts of it are, I feel, the best prose I have ever written in my life."[18] In an interview as late as 1976 Jones cited *Some Came Running* as his favorite work.

Jones did not often complain openly about the critical beating he took for *Some Came Running*. Whining does not seem to have been part of his repertoire. Yet he took it all seriously enough. In a letter of December 2, 1959, to his friend William Styron, he offers sympathy for Styron's anxiety about the fate of an upcoming book by sharing his feelings, still fresh from the experience. "I can sympathize with you, knowing your toenails, about what the critics will do to you in the spring. But they don't really bother me much, I guess. Maybe because they'll never be able to hit me any harder, at any rate, than they did with SOME CAME RUNNING. When you get hit that hard there is nowhere left to go, but up."[19]

On the other hand, Jones never turned against *Eternity*. From first to last he seemed truly grateful for what he had learned in the making of it, what he had grasped, and what he had been given by its success. In a piece written for Maurice Dolbier's "Books and Authors" in the *New York Herald Tribune*, "What NBA Means to Some Past Winners," Jones was straightforward and simply candid about what the National Book Award, given to him for *Eternity*, had meant to him:

In my own particular case, because the novel with which I won it was such a commercial success (totally beyond the expectations of myself or my publishers), I think it gave to me a certain literary status and prestige which might not otherwise have been accorded to me. To have a commercial success often appears to make it harder for a novelist to receive any literary acclaim, so in this sense I think the Award did help me greatly. On the other hand, I cannot honestly say that it has helped my other work to be regarded more seriously by book-reviewers and critics.[20]

Jones gives every sign of being well aware of the growth and change in himself, and he never seems to look back too wistfully on what he once had been or might have been. Mostly he looked forward. He rejoiced in the making and doing of the work at hand, and he was not so modest, privately, that he was reluctant to make considerable claims for it. For example, in a letter to his friend, the young novelist Michael Mewshaw, Jones says of *Whistle*, even as he was working on it, that "I'm very pleased and very confident that it will be a major American work. Taken with the two other books as a trilogy (ETERNITY and LINE) I think it will be even more than that. If I can maintain the level I have maintained so far, I think the Trilogy has a good chance to become one of the major works of the English language."[21]

When James Jones died, and in the three successive waves of public attention which helped to shape the general outlines of a critical consensus, it was agreed that he had indeed acquired a permanent place in the American literary hierarchy. And the fact of that agreement would itself be enough to justify a retelling of his life story. But there are other good

Drawing by Jones, 1975

OLD SOLDIERS NEVER DIE.

THEY WRITE NOVELS.

BLACKSTONE
Jan 17, 1975.

With sister, Mary Ann ("Tink")

reasons to examine the life and art of James Jones and to consider his place in the story of our literature.

One of these reasons is that the story and direction of our literature has changed, even as our national life, our *way of life*, has changed—sharply, perhaps radically—since World War II, and that most of this changing took place coterminously with the boundaries of his writing career. Jones was acutely aware, at times presciently, of the changes as they were happening, and he recorded and reflected them in his works, clearly and maybe more accurately than most of the other writers of his generation. Perhaps Norman Mailer, Jones's friend, could be advanced as, at the very least, an equally sentient witness to the changing times. These changes have been, after all, Mailer's main theme. But there is a serious difference. Indomitably urban and Jewish, formally well educated, at once a hip intellectual and a streetwise pitchman, Mailer can almost be said to *represent* the changes that have come to pass. He is an apostle of the new and, as such, has next to no connection, no roots, in the older America with its own vanishing style and traditions, out of which Jones came. Mailer surely sought to uncover those roots, insofar as he can imagine them, in *Executioner's Song*. And Jones himself had tried to expose them, the rot at the heart of them, and to bid the old ways farewell in *Some Came Running*. But the two writers had less essentially in common than they realized. Early on Jones recognized they were headed off in very different directions. As Jones wrote to Mailer, in March of 1956: "We both have our work to do, our paths to follow, and they appear to be increasingly divergent." Jones was a man divided by time and by events in a way that Mailer is not. And Jones was conscious of the inner tension created by this kind of duality, this delicate balance of self-division. Jones explored and exploited his inner conflict in all of his work. Part of him was always the small town child, the archetypal inheritor of the American heartland towns, which had not changed greatly since the childhood of the previous generation of American writers. That had, in fact, changed only superficially since the days of the childhood of Mark Twain. One of the earliest surviving creations of James Jones is a letter addressed to his Aunt Mollie and Uncle Guy in California, dated November 23, 1932, from the old 400 East Walnut Street address in Robinson. Its text reads as follows:

> I don't know if you remember me or not. I am your nephew, Jim. I'm sorry I haven't written to you before now but I've been too darn busy.

I carry papers in the morning and then go to school to work on my lessons. After school I play football till it's dark. When I get home I'm pretty sleepy.[23]

One of the principal reasons that rural and small town America, in all its regional diversity, was set to a lazy, slow-motion metronome rhythm of change during Jones's childhood and youth was the impact of the Great Depression. Even amid the widespread suffering and discontent of those days, the far-flung towns of America struggled to preserve themselves, their values, and whatever could be preserved against ruin and change. But everything *was* changed—and suddenly—once World War II came to involve the United States. It was that older America that Jones left behind when he enlisted in the Army in late 1939. It was the old, small (190,000 men) Regular Army that he joined, the Army of canvas leggings, the wide-brimmed, high-crowned campaign hat, and the beautifully made and balanced Springfield rifle (U.S. Rifle, Caliber 30, 1903-A3). Within a year, the first draftees would begin to arrive and fill up the old and new outfits. The new soldier would go to war wearing green fatigues and the new steel pot helmet with its plastic liner, carrying the new Garand rifle, the semi-automatic M1. Thus the Army, itself, changed quickly and permanently while he was in it. And it was a very different America from the one he had known and remembered that he discovered when he returned as a wounded combat veteran and a grown man in May of 1943. His letters and notebooks, his poems and stories, from those days and later, dealing with that period, speak of a sense of deep shock at his homecoming to a greatly altered homefront. He brought with him the sudden and terrible truth of war which had come to him in Guadalcanal. Recovering from his wound in Guadalcanal, he wrote (January 28, 1943) to his brother, Jeff, what the experience of combat had taught him: "I also learned that in spite of all the training you get and precautions you take to keep yourself alive, it's largely a matter of luck that decides whether or not you get killed."[24] This knowledge would later be the core of truth in his combat novel—*The Thin Red Line*. From Letterman General Hospital in San Francisco, where he stayed briefly before being sent on to Kennedy Hospital near Memphis, he wrote of his annoyance at the persistence of the Army's system of caste and class at home. "It's rather odd to get back where officers [are] condescending," he wrote Jeff on May 22, 1943. "On the front they're all pretty good guys; back here they have their usual privileges and superiority."[25] In

Memphis he and his buddies were suddenly and fully involved in the life of wartime America. As he remembered and wrote to Burroughs Mitchell: "It was a wild time then, we were the first batch from overseas to come here. . . . Most of us drew 9 to 14 months back pay at one crack. The Peabody cocktail lounge was clustered with dames out to help us spend it like grapes on a vine."[26] *Whistle* would tell that story.

By the time he wrote *WWII* and *Whistle* he had fairly well sorted out the various elements that added up to his sense of shock. He could distinguish between those parts which came from the sharp contrast between the veterans' experience of combat and the civilians' innocence of it, what he described in *WWII* as "the vast and sanguine confidence of the home 'front' after mid-1943." He and the others were shocked by "the richness of everybody." "True that the thirties had been lean years, and that everybody was happy to be back at work full swing, and that everybody was belaboring it for all they were worth. . . . But the sheer magnitude of it shocked. And there were moments when it seemed they were truly making it off our red meat and bone."[27] Though he loathed the sexual hypocrisies of heartland America (as he perceived them then), Jones was also shocked by the new morality, writing that "it was clear enough to any eye that had been away abroad that the mores and morals of the nation's middle class were swiftly undergoing a sea change. The wild gaiety and rollicking despair that characterized the towns and cities near the camps certainly helped this."[28] That despair, hidden behind gaiety, had long haunted him. In an interview with Barbara Bannon of *Publishers Weekly*, he described it explicitly. "Jones believes 'there was a lot of despair floating around in those years,' " Bannon wrote. " 'FDR never saw fit to tangle with it and it never got in the newspapers but it was there.' "[29]

Jones's feelings about the changed morality, what would eventually turn into "the sexual revolution," were mixed, sufficiently so that his wife felt it necessary to explain this to Hugh Moffett of *Life* magazine. "They [the critics] don't understand Jim," she said. "Jim is a Midwestern square. *Widow-Maker* is not a dirty book. It's puritanical. He's against all those characters he has in there."[30]

Like the earlier generation of American writers, the modern masters—Anderson, Hemingway, Steinbeck, Faulkner, Fitzgerald, Wolfe, all of whom Jones read eagerly and early and altogether unsystematically, with at first no other purpose than the pure pleasure of it—Jones developed a double vision about the world he had grown up in, a love-hate relationship. No question that he hated the complacency, the hypocrisy, the petty bigotries, the nearly invincible ignorance and small-mindedness and meanness of spirit when he encountered these things. As he did. And he wrote about them. And spoke out about them. As early as 1940, writing to Jeff from the 18th AB Squadron at Wheeler Field in Hawaii, as much for philosophical as personal reasons he could say that "Robinson holds nothing for me but a bitter taste."[31] Writing to Maxwell Perkins, in 1946, Jones contrasted the unhappiness of Robinson and New York: "Here you are unhappy because everybody knows you; in New York you are unhappy because nobody knows you."[32] But there was much that he loved, also. And later in his life, when he was much more sophisticated and worldly wise, when he had seen a great deal of the world, that love stood out in strong contrast to the stereotypical attitudes expressed by so many of his peers, close friends among them. For that was a time when many other American writers, closely allied with the academic intellectuals, were vociferous in their denunciation of nearly everything American, when it was completely conventional (and safe) to affect to despise America's present and to ridicule America's past, and to be well rewarded for taking that stance. But Jones's affection for what was good and honorable and worth preserving in American culture remained undiminished in his consciousness, kept intact through many outward and inner changes. His fierce integrity forbade him to deny his own roots, which were not, in fact, except by the most extreme radical definitions, "conservative," but were deeply set in an older independent, and basically populist tradition. As early as spring of 1947, Jones was deeply worried about the growing tension between the United States and the Soviet Union. In a letter to Perkins he said, "I'm quite concerned we will have to fight Russia before it is ended, and I am remembering the hell it was too, as I write this." But he had by then read Arthur Koestler's *Darkness at Noon*, and that had reinforced his hopes for, if not his unquestioning belief in, this country. "I've seen so many things wrong with this country," he added to Perkins, "yet with all of it I sure as hell wouldn't trade it for Russia."[33] He was telling Burroughs Mitchell the plain truth when he wrote in 1951: "If the anarchists weren't Anarchists, complete with party and organization, I think I'd be tempted to join them."[34] He was speaking out of that American tradition when he wrote to M. J. Lasky in Berlin, editor of *Der Monat*, that he did not wish to be involved in any propaganda. "As a matter of fact, Mr. Lasky," he wrote, "there is nothing I detest worse than a writer who writes propaganda—whether he be Russian, Chinese, American, or Eskimo."[35] There was the telegram of May 23, 1960, sent to William Styron in Rome, concerning a petition written by Wallace Stegner, Blair Fuller, Ben Johnson, and Styron, a statement against capital punishment. Jones refused to sign it, though he offered to pass it on to others who probably would. His position was "I agree in principle but do not like the tone."[36]

Jones even allowed himself certain occasional moments of unabashed, old-fashioned patriotism—if by that word we mean love of a country and of its people, love of its best traditions. In a 1962 interview the interviewer says to him, "Your people on the whole are fairly crude individuals. As a matter of fact, some of them are outright louts, and yet they speak all the time about dignity. Why is that?"

"Because they are Americans."[37]

It was not at all accidental that when Jones went looking for a publisher, he went first to Charles Scribner's Sons. Scribner's was the publisher of Hemingway, Fitzgerald, and Wolfe. He sought out there as his first editor the celebrated Maxwell Perkins, from whom (before the editor's death in 1947) he received encouragement, editorial guidance, and— probably more significant—a symbolic laying on of hands. It was a deliberate, conscious (*self-conscious*, if you will) gesture designed to link himself directly with the great tradition of American letters as Jones perceived it. Even so, from the beginning, much that was old and honored was already fading into shadows, already changing. The new and different was beginning to appear on the scene when Jones arrived at Scribner's. Hemingway seems to have sensed this acutely. His fury against Jones and *From Here to Eternity* is obvious in a series of letters Hemingway exchanged with Charles Scribner, Jr., shortly after *From Here to Eternity* had appeared and Hemingway had read it. There are moments in these letters when Hemingway seems to be completely out of control, obscenely if not insanely jealous. With the kind of terrible irony that history and hindsight can afford, it is chilling to read Hemingway's contemptuous description of Jones as suicidal and his prediction that Jones will sooner or later commit suicide.[38]

It does not seem likely that Jones ever saw any of these letters or knew anything much about them, but he never was an unmitigated admirer of

In Vietnam for research on Viet Journal

Hemingway, whom he faulted chiefly on grounds that would have hurt Hemingway the most—his honesty. Jones felt that Hemingway had not told the whole truth about any number of things, including the nature of courage and the experience of combat. And that—not telling the whole truth and nothing but the truth, as far and as deeply as an artist could perceive it—was the gravest fault of all as far as Jones was concerned, a fault not to be disguised or overcome by Hemingway's virtuoso artistry or by all the felicities of his famous style. In a 1946 letter to Perkins, he tried to explain that he was not "set against Hemingway." "I think he is a fine writer," Jones wrote, "but to date I have discovered only two writers whom I can take all the way, or at least nearly so; and these are Scott Fitzgerald and Tom Wolfe."[39] And he wrote to Scribner's editor John Hall Wheelock in 1947 that it was his aspiration to combine in his own work "the spiritual insight and poetry of Tom Wolfe with the pellucid clarity and reality of life moving [that] Hemingway has."[40] Years later, in an *Esquire* piece about bullfighting at Pamplona, "Letter Home: Sons of Hemingway," Jones could reduce all his complex doubts and reservations to one simple question: "What had he done to us all with his big masculine bullshit?"[41]

If Jones was self-consciously an American traditionalist, he was also (and with an equally old-fashioned American attitude) an innovator, one who was eager to experiment and one who was open to the innovative and experimental in the work of others. When *Catch-22* came along, he read it early, liked it a lot, and went out of his way to tell others about it. There is a letter to Burroughs Mitchell in which Jones describes the novel, judging that it is "a remarkable and very good book."[42] Among the letters preserved in the James Jones Archives of the Humanities Research Center at the University of Texas, there is one to Jones in Paris from Herman Gollob, then a young editor at Atheneum, who expresses gratitude to Jones for earlier kindness and generosity to him. It is a letter of introduction to a young writer, on his way to Paris, who is eager to meet Jones—a young writer whom Gollob is sure Jones will like even as he is sure Jones will enjoy his work: Donald Barthelme.[43] And there stands a momentary meeting of old and new in our literary history, a brief intersection of quite different forces: the one (Barthelme) a *New Yorker* writer for whom character was less important than costume, for whom stylish verbal felicity was the silk purse every sow's ear yearned for; the other (Jones) for whom depth and dimension of characterization was fiction's coin of the realm, for the sake of which even style, and certainly all buck-and-wing showboating, was expendable. Barthelme was a new writer, chic and clever and assertively experimental, a writer for whom language and style are far more important than any experience and by whom experience itself is viewed as stereotypical, life being imagined as a sequence of clichés. To Jones, representative of an older tradition, fidelity to experience is the primary test of truth, and the telling of truth is the whole point of the art. Experiments in narrative prose must be real, yet complex enough, well disguised enough to be missed by those who can recognize the original only in bold superficial signs. That Gollob believed Jones would enjoy the young man and his work speaks volumes, for Jones. It says at the least (which his whole life bears out) that he was a generous man, open- and large-minded. That Donald Barthelme wanted to meet James Jones while he was in Paris says that by then Jones had become something of a cultural institution. In any case, Jones, who had known Maxwell Perkins professionally if briefly, had some belief in the efficacy of the laying on of hands. All his life he was generous and helpful to other writers, especially the beginners. In a letter to Walter J. Minton of Putnam's, supporting the value of a first novel by a young writer, *Never the Same Again* (1956) by Gerald Tesch, which, it seems, dealt with some homosexual experiences, Jones says: "I'm not especially hot for homosexuality. I *am* hot to get the *truth* told; about *any*thing; any*where*, in this country of ours. You and I both know how very little of it *does* get told, especially if it has anything to do with sex, homo or otherwise."[44] A fortnight later, having produced a blurb for Minton, he wanted a copy of the galleys: "I've made the goddamned comment for you; how about sending me the goddamned galleys? I want them."[45]

The story of Jones, as writer, is larger, more emblematic and inclusive, then, than the story of a man who wrote one undeniable masterpiece or even of the man who wrote the finest works about World War II. It is a story of old and new, the account of an artist who was actively involved and engaged in the life of our times. When Jones arrived on the scene, the old ways of American publishing were represented by Charles Scribner's Sons, a small family-owned corporation where the editors were gentlemen and where, yes, tea was served in the offices each afternoon, and where, to survive and turn a profit, advances were small, and parsimony with authors was company policy. The old ways of American publishing were giving way to new forces, chiefly the sudden explosion in the postwar years of mass market paperback publication (so that this subsidiary right soon became crucial to the success or failure of hardcover publishing), the book clubs, the blockbuster, feast or famine economics. And as the new ways triumphed, the old American dream of the happy marriage of serious and popular literature began to die. Norman Mailer stated it flatly in a 1963 piece, "The Big Bite," for *Esquire*: "One could not make one's living writing good novels any more."[46]

James Jones may well prove to be one of the last of our major novelists to try to bring these sundered forms together, succeeding several times. He earned a living, and a good one, as an honest novelist. He married happily —once and, as it happens, wisely and well. He raised a family, lived well, and when he died, left behind an adequate estate, above and beyond the incalculable inheritance of his published works. But he was near the end of something in American literary history. Like Faulkner's Dilsey, he had seen the first and the last of it.

It should be mentioned, briefly, that Jones was also among the last, together with a few others of his generation (like Shelby Foote and John Cheever and J. D. Salinger) *not* to have been exposed to a full-scale, formal college education. A generation earlier, *most* American writers were self-educated and proud of it. In an exchange of letters with a Tulane professor of English, who had written an intelligent article about *From Here to Eternity*, Jones wrote: "I seem to get the impression that you see me as an uneducated child of the slums or something who had a mysterious talent for writing pretty much the truth without having to think hard about it. Such is not the case, though I admit unblushingly that I have not had the dubious (to a writer) benefit of a thorough college education."[47]

But with the end of World War II came the G.I. Bill and its opportunities for veterans. Jones himself took advantage of these for one semester at New York University in 1945; and in January of 1946 he wrote to his sister Mary Ann that he was seriously considering going to study at either the University of Florida or at Duke.[48]

With the G.I. Bill and the mass publication and marketing of paperback books came also the study first of modern writing, then of contemporary literature, in the academies. And soon, too, came the writers, writers in residence, then regular writer-teachers into the academy. The network of associations of American writers with the American academies, and with the intellectuals who staff and manage them, remains to be sorted out. No one knows what it all adds up to. Yet no one, not even the most enthusiastic supporter of writing programs and the academic life, will claim that all of the effects have been beneficial. One thing is certain— where once there were many self-educated American writers, there are precious few today. Jones lived to see this happen. He witnessed the triumph of the intellectuals. More than that, when he returned from Europe to live in the United States in 1974, he worked a full year as visiting professor and writer in residence at Florida International University. And there was some talk of his returning to teaching again once *Whistle* was finished.

Above and beyond all things literary, Jones's story is more generally emblematic. For it is also the story, as seen through the life and character of an alert and sensitive individual of an America that is first fixed in its own past, as if drunk with the sweet wine of nostalgia, and then all of a sudden takes fire from all sides with change. It is hard for those who lived through it to remember back before World War II, to recall that world so different that it might have been dreamed or only visited, like a foreign country. The experience of World War II—the time leading up to our entry into the war, the duration, and the immediate postwar years—can be understood not merely as a time of transition or of the gradual transformation of society, but as a time of the most complex and radical changes. Many elements of mundane life, most now so familiar that it is difficult to imagine life without them, were introduced into the culture in the years following World War II. Not only television, whose direct influence on all aspects of American life (including the art of story-telling) was immediate and enormous and whose power has grown to immeasurable proportions, but also such ordinary things as the long-playing record (and the consequent development of high quality audio systems), extensive and rapid photojournalism, synthetic fibers and fabrics, the supermarket, the shopping center—these last two designed to serve the needs of the suddenly burgeoning suburbs—all are essentially postwar phenomena. As are motels and interstate highways. Prior to the war and during the war, most domestic travel was accomplished on the passenger trains. The highway and freeway culture and the mobility that goes with it, taken in conjunction with the inexorably spreading world of airlines and airports, a world of many and speedy choices, are postwar innovations. All held back first by the Depression, then by the national concentration on winning the war.

And in the war and the years immediately following, there was a change in the federal nature of the American republic. The emergency New Deal years had given impetus to increasing federalism. But it was the war and the postwar years that changed both the nature and the understanding of the complex relationship between the central government in Washington and the governments of the states. Technically, prior to World War II, deriving from the gradual enlargement of federal powers during the New Deal years and by and through the Supreme Court's reinterpretation of the meaning and implications of the Fourteenth Amendment, the relationship between Washington and the states had already changed. However, it now seems significant that the really major changes in federalism—as, for example, the Supreme Court's unanimous 1954 decision on the issue of de jure segregation in the public schools—did not happen, were not seriously envisioned (except by the beleaguered minority), indeed were not considered possible prior to World War II.

Where did James Jones fit into all this? Well, as soon as he could, in the late 1940s, he hit the road, traveling restlessly back and forth across his newfound country—to Florida, Arizona, Colorado, California, New Mexico, New York. He was on the road and on the move well before the Beat Generation discovered the joys of freedom and mobility. As soon as he earned any money from his first novel, he performed the great American postwar gesture—he built himself a house. And he filled it with wonderful new gadgetry, including elaborate and expensive audio components. Like most Americans, Jones had mixed feelings about the new directions of his government. He was always a defender of what we now call human rights and an unsentimental champion of underdogs of all kinds. It was perfectly natural that early on he should seriously consider writing a novel about what he then called "the Negro problem." Early and late he contributed to organizations concerned with civil rights. But, at the same time, he saw the growing bureaucracy, which inevitably accompanied the growth of federal power, as a grave and present danger to liberty, to what he called inclusively "individuality." And he greatly feared the increasing "mechanization of society," saw it as the most serious danger faced by mankind. In an interview following a reading in Frankfurt from the manuscript of *The Thin Red Line* on November 10, 1960, he told a reporter: "If they drop the bomb or don't makes little difference. We can't overcome the mechanization of society."[49] Seven years later he was quoted in *Life* as saying,

Publicity photo outside trailer, 1951

On return to the United States, Sagaponack, 1974

"Bureaucracy and technocracy are going to take away whatever individualism we've got left."[50] Like most Americans, James Jones looked for justice and equality, but not at the expense of individual liberty—a complex, if familiar position, more deeply emotional than intellectual. In this inner conflict he was closer to his countrymen than most intellectuals, conservative or liberal.

The changing in and of America, in large and vague things and in small, sharp details of daily life, is a story James Jones witnessed and felt deeply and tried to record in his work even as it was happening. Like the country he loved and criticized and the people he loved to write about, Jones was quite suddenly thrust forward into a different world, a world at war, one where illusions and not truths were the first casualties. Thousands of young Americans died in the war. But millions more of them left a littered wealth of old (and sometimes comforting) illusions strewn behind them like the expendable and inessential items of equipment they threw aside as they went into combat. By luck and by accident and by dint of unceasing hard labor, for it was never really *easy* for him and he distrusted easy things, Jones became a significant spokesman for disillusioned America. But—and here, I believe, is the special quality of this artist which gave to everything he created the unmistakable crystal ring of authority and truth telling—he never dispensed with his honest innocence, at least the clear memory of it, when he discarded his illusions. In 1953 in *The Nation*, he argued that it was necessary for the best American writers to *grow up*. "I am convinced," he wrote, "that you can't be a big writer unless you stop being a child and just become a big man. I hope someday I'll be able to do it."[51] He aged, he grew in wisdom and stature, but to the end, in spite of his earlier wishes, he managed to keep alive and well in memory, in consciousness, the image of the boy he had been. That is, he never wholly renounced the youth even as he outgrew him and finally lost him. He says it beautifully, and exactly, at the end of *Viet Journal* where, he feels, he can bid his own lost image of himself farewell.

That night an old friend drove me out to the airport to say good-by. We sat in the lounge and talked about the old days at the university in Manoa Valley, when I had gone there. But we ticketholders rode out to the plane in a bus, and I could not see the airport building to wave good-by. The airport itself looked entirely foreign. As tired as the others, I climbed the steep stairs. I had come back hoping to meet a certain twenty-year-old boy, walking along Kalakaua Avenue in a "gook" shirt, perhaps, but I had not seen him.[52]

Boy and man, Jones never lost his energetic interest, his continual curiosity, the freshness of his vision. It was these qualities, coupled with the rigor of his integrity, which defined the character of his lifework. John Hall Wheelock said it to Jones in a letter with all of a poet's economical and refined simplicity: "You experience everything, dear Jim, as if for the first time."[53]

PART TWO
· · ·
BOY TO MAN

•   •   •

ROBINSON is the county seat of Crawford County and lies in south-eastern Illinois, not very far from the Wabash and the Indiana state line. In fact the nearest place of any good size is Terre Haute. Named for Senator John McCracken Robinson (1794–1843), it is set amid farm country, among woods and slight hills, and might have remained a truly rural town, like Marshall to the north, had it not been for the oil discovered and exploited in the area shortly after the turn of the century. In and around Marshall, the wells were exhausted by the time America entered the First World War. But the Robinson wells remained active, and a large Ohio Oil (now called Marathon Oil) refinery was established there. James Jones was born into a family which had acquired some oil money and the sense of respectability that is the reward of good fortune. In the remarkable entry in *Twentieth Century Authors: A Biographical Dictionary of Modern Literature*, Jones was at once frank and cynical about this, describing his family as one "that had lived in that county for several generations, and thus had achieved the social respect and position such families can get only by living in the same place a long time without going broke." He mentions the family farm where his grandfather grew up, adding: "There is still an old family cemetery with big pine trees where the old farm was. Oil was discovered on the farm and my grandfather became a lawyer and moved to town." His roots were deep, and he was conscious of them. In a letter to a woman who had written in 1956 to ask if he might be writing a book about the Civil War, he replied that he was not ready yet for such a thing, though someday he might be. He added that he had a great uncle who was buried in "Grave No. 90 of the 113th Iowa at Gettysburg."[2] And he claimed kin on both sides, including some who fought for Nathan Bedford Forrest and others who rode with Morgan's Raiders.

Success followed his grandfather into town, where he had his offices in what was called the Jones Building. According to Jones, he helped to finance the research and development of insulin and bought and maintained an elegant three-story, columned old mansion on West Main Street, which *Newsweek* writer Robert E. Cantwell described as "the most impressive in town."[3] This big house eventually came into the hands of Jones's uncle, Charles Jones, himself a successful lawyer, who named it Westward Home, had stationery printed up with a picture of the mansion on it, and lived there until his death in an auto accident in late 1956. Now nothing remains of the house except the tall columns standing like a mild midwestern parody of a Mississippi Delta ruin.

There is something vaguely southern about the old house, just as there is something almost southern about the accent and speech of that part of Illinois, about the manners and what has come to be called the life-style. Jones was conscious of this, and what he wrote for *Ford Times* about Marshall applies also to Robinson, that it was "a curious combination of Eastern frugality and taciturnity, and Southern laziness and easy-going living."[4] When Mr. and Mrs. Charles Jones celebrated their twenty-fifth wedding anniversary, in November of 1954, the *Robinson Argus* stressed the southern connection in its coverage of the social event:

Their colonial home had an atmosphere of the days in times before "Gone With the Wind" with two colored servants, one of whom was a colored boy from Shelbyville, Tenn. His great grandfather was a slave of Mrs. Jones' great grandfather and this boy came to be chef

Jones's maternal grandfather Blessing

Jones's maternal grandmother Blessing

Jones's mother as a very young woman

OPPOSITE: *Earliest photo of Jones as a baby*

Jones's father, Dr. Ramon Jones, as a young man

At age fifteen, when he was a "four-eyed" schoolboy, 1936

for the festive occasion, cooking and serving a 33 pound Tennessee ham, turkeys, shrimp, lobster, clams, beaten biscuits and hot rolls.[5]

James Jones did not attend the party, which resulted in some aggravation of already strained family feelings.

Jones's father, Dr. Ramon Jones, was a dentist who had less good luck than his brother Charles. Of his father Jones wrote this for *Twentieth Century Authors*:

> My father went to Northwestern and became a dentist instead of a lawyer because he wanted to get out of school quicker so he could get married sooner. He would have preferred to be a lawyer. My mother came from Iowa, of an old German family there which had migrated from New York, and was considered a great beauty locally. She would have preferred to remain a great beauty. My parents were, I think, too much in love ever to be happily married, although I did not understand this then. My father took to drink and my mother to religion.

Jones goes on to describe the atmosphere of his home life as one "of hot emotions and boiling recriminations covered with a thin but resilient skin of gentility." And this tension was soon increased by the death of the grandfather and by financial disasters.

> We were forced to move. This was when I was a junior in high school. As a small boy I had accepted our family's social position without ever questioning it or even realizing it was there; I soon learned social prestige, while a very important thing, was still a very ephemeral one, and that if there is any permanency in this world at all, that is not it.[6]

The Depression was not kind to small town dentists or to other skilled professionals who dealt in services and often had to wait a long time to be paid or to be content with barter payments. Nor did alcoholism and social decline help Dr. Jones's practice. One result of all this was that James Jones was encouraged to join the Army rather than to go to college. His older brother, Jeff, popular and successful in high school, a good student and an athlete, had come along twelve years earlier when things were good. But it was not possible for James Jones, or for his younger sister, Mary Ann, to consider a college education. As a whaling ship had been Herman Melville's Harvard, so the U.S. Army would have to do for Jones.

There are any number of people in Robinson who remember Jones as a child (or profess to), though time and hindsight have surely shaped their recollections. And it must be difficult to isolate miscellaneous early memories from the later ones—of Jones coming back from the war and then of the long writing of *From Here to Eternity*, followed by its sudden overwhelming success. Then came the half dozen years when, now a successful indeed famous writer, he went to live up the road in Marshall and to write *Some Came Running*. Feelings toward him were (and are) mixed, although by 1969, when Rand McNally put together its *Illinois: Guide & Gazetteer*, Jones was safely in residence elsewhere and could be properly claimed as the town's most important native son: "Robinson is the birthplace of James Jones, author of *From Here to Eternity*, published in 1951. He wrote part of the book while living in a writers' colony near here, supported by the late Mrs. Lowney Handy. He later bought a house in Marshall, Clark County, but more recently has lived in France."[7] Some sense of the mixed blessings of small town living, at once supportive and implacably inquisitive, is evident in the following page-one story from the *Robinson Argus*, August 31, 1950:

JAMES JONES LEAVES FOR CONFERENCE
WITH NEW YORK PUBLISHERS

James Jones, local author, left Thursday for New York City for a final conference with the House of Scribner concerning his forthcoming novel scheduled to be published in February 1951. Jim will spend the Labor Day week end as the houseguest of Burroughs Mitchell, at the latter's country home in Dutchess County, N.Y.

We need not depend on the selective memories of others, however; for Jones has left a good record of his own mixed feelings about himself and his youth. In letters, in interviews, and in some of the best of the stories collected in *The Ice-Cream Headache and Other Stories*, there is strong evidence of the conflicts and contradictions which helped to shape his character. In a 1951 article in *Life* by A. B. C. Whipple, he described himself as "a shy kid with glasses."[8] In the Leslie Hanscom interview

("The Writer Speaks"), Hanscom wonders how a man like Jones ended up as a writer. "You're somebody who appears to be designed by nature to exert physical strength," Hanscom says, "and yet you have undertaken to pursue the four-eyed profession of writing. What happened?"

"I think it was because, as you said, four-eyed," Jones answers. "I think it was because I had to wear glasses when I was little."[9] Besides suffering from being shy and having to wear glasses, Jones was short, thin, and physically immature for his age. As he wrote to Burroughs Mitchell, "I was little and thin and didn't fill out till the army."[10] In that same letter, in which the subject is sports and athletic ability, Jones says that he never did well in school in the team sports which mattered so much for popularity and self-esteem. He says he was laughed at when he tried to play baseball. His reaction was to try all the harder, but soon he was trying too hard to be able to play well or gracefully. His brother Jeff had been an outstanding athlete and had been voted Most Popular. It was a hard act to follow. Jones confesses to his brother that he himself was "considered class prick."[11] Later, in a letter accompanying a manuscript of Jeff's, which Jones, with characteristic generosity, was recommending to Burroughs Mitchell's attention, Jones wrote: "He grew up before our family losts [*sic*] its money and its social position, whereas I came along 12 years later and was forced to fight for my pride from the first time I entered school."[12] There was another side to Jones—the fighter. There are hints and clues of some serious behavior problems, of fights, taking dangerous dares, something about pushing another boy through a glass store window; he concealed his shyness behind a banty rooster bravado, a hair-trigger temper, and indomitable pride. Jones remembered himself as the black sheep of the family.[13] He also had a reputation for being fearless, something Jeff had complimented him for and something which Jones felt needed the corrective of plain truth. "I haven't got guts," he wrote, "I'm just more afraid of what people will think of me than I am of getting hurt a little."[14]

To this clash of forces in a complex child was added a well-above-average intelligence. As much to his own surprise as well as that of others, he had tested as a "genius" in the eighth grade.[15] And he could report with some pride that he had made "the highest grades" on the battery of tests administered by the Army Air Force.[16] Similarly, when he transferred into the infantry, Jones was evidently under some real pressure to apply for Officers Candidate School because of outstanding test scores.

If we turn to the evidence and implication of the John Slade stories published in *The Ice-Cream Headache*, stories Jones claimed as autobiographical and that tend to conform to the known details of his youth even while adding more information, we discover other characteristics and other forces at work within him. In the stories of Slade as a child—"Just Like the Girl," "The Valentine," "A Bottle of Cream," "The Tennis Game," and, even though the protagonist is here called Tom Dylan, "The Ice-Cream Headache"—we are presented with a more complete picture than anywhere else of the family, a "Faulknerian" family, as Tom Dylan conceived them. Jones told Willie Morris about his mother: "He found her domineering, cruel and deceitful; he called her a 'dwarf' and said she had 'the mind of a mole.'"[17] And in the introductory note to "The Tennis Game" Jones wrote that the story is "an interesting study of male masochism of which there appears to be a great deal in my generation, brought on of course by mothers like the mother in the story."[18] But within the imaginary context, in the texture of the stories, she is at once more terrible and more pathetic than the stereotypical bad Mom. In "Just Like the Girl" she forces the young boy to spy on his drunken father, using his fear and the threatened loss of her love. He ends up much as might be expected, contemptuous of them both and of himself and finally incapable of bearing the weight of confused guilt except by the art of adroit rationalization. In "The Tennis Game" and "The Ice-Cream Headache" it is sex—sexual hunger and frustration made the more acute by enforced ignorance and imposed hypocrisy—that drives the boy wild. Yet in these same stories the protagonist continues to endure, through the exercise of imagination and of secrecy, what the narrator of "Tennis Game" calls "the old sad fatalistic secret tickle of almost hurtful pleasure."[19] He works out elaborate and imaginative solitary games, together with active, if ordinary sexual fantasies, to counteract his constant rage and frustration, to feed his insatiable pride. Tom Dylan is old enough and sufficiently honest in introspection to think he understands the essential flaw of that "Faulknerian" family.

What the Dylan family had suffered from was, mainly, pride. Good old *human* pride, the stuff that made the spheres revolve and the world go round, as *humans* liked to say so much of it. But which also caused more stubborn bitchery, hardheaded meanness, hate, destruction, murder and organized mayhem than could be found anywhere else in the animal kingdom all put together. Good old old-fashioned American, Middlewestern, kill-me-but-I'll-never-budge pride.[20]

Tom Dylan/John Slade survive not so much because they escape the doom of false pride, for although they are aware of it and its power over them, it is an inheritance they cannot really choose to reject. Rather they are armored with the power of the imagination, cultivated in part by constant reading (Jones was a voracious reader all his life) and by the creation of a satisfactory fantasy life made from the raw materials of deeply felt experience. But paradoxically, it is knowledge and awareness of the truth, of the fact that there is truth to be ascertained in a world riddled with lies and self-deceptions, that strengthens them, saves them from withdrawal from sanity. They may not be able to help themselves, to tell the truth as they understand it; but the knowledge of it is secret power. The child is not deceived. Here, in "The Tennis Game," John Slade considers his mother's furious assertion of the work ethic at the expense of his childhood pleasures:

> And because, as she said when she got mad, her son was going to learn to work because it built character and was good for his soul—and he was going to learn it if it killed the both of them. But the real truth was that she couldn't stand to see him outdoors playing and having fun while she herself had to clean house and cook. She just couldn't stand it, he could tell by the look on her face, and so the whole thing was no more than one big damned lie. One of those grownup lies, that grownups told each other and pretended to believe and that children because they were little had to accept and pretend to believe too, because they could not argue back.[21]

This boy, under whatever name, also manages to endure by means of well-preserved secrecy and by an enormous effort of the will, this latter itself a form of pride. We can see and feel this at the ending of "The Valentine," where the lonely, lovesick John Slade, having spent all his savings from the paper route to buy an expensive box of candy for the beautiful Margaret Simpson, leaves the candy on her desk for her and hides in the cloakroom, from where he watches her react to his gift as a joke. He is swept by terrible waves of sickness and shame, but somehow or other he must return to the classroom when the bell rings. "When the bell rang, he forced himself to walk to the door and to his desk and sat down, trying hard not to look at anybody."[22]

If these stories present a painful childhood and a complex, self-conscious child creating a gnarled image of hatred and of self-contempt, they also demonstrate a completely sentient awareness of place, a rendering of the sense of large things and small which, in the keen fidelity of evocation, comes close to being an expression of love. This is especially true of "The Valentine" where scenes in Woolworth's and at the newsstand pleased Jones enough to say so in the introductory note to that story. There, too, an early morning ride to deliver papers is suddenly rich and complicated with joy.

> Outside it was steely cold and the handlebars and sprocket of his bike creaked with frost when he moved them. The air burned his nose like dry ice, and as he tucked the scarf up over it and put on his goggles, his eyes were already watering. The freezing cold air flushing the last threads of sleepiness and reluctance out of his mind, he took off on his bike, giving himself joyously up to, and embracing happily, the discomfort which always made him feel important and as though he were accomplishing something, riding the bike downtown along deserted streets of darkened houses where nothing moved or shone and people slept except for a few boys like himself, scattered across town, converging on the Newsstand where the city papers would already have been picked up by the owner off the train.[23]

Reviewing this collection of stories for the *New York Times Book Review*, John Thompson concluded that "Jones is incapable of anything but total loyalty to his own experience as a man, as an American, as a Middle Westerner, as a child of the Depression and of World War II; as the son of an American mother, and, may Heaven help us all, of an American father."[24]

It seems likely that a large part of any writer's basic equipment for the practice of his craft is in place and intact by childhood's end. What becomes of it, and of the artist, depends on circumstance and luck as much as discipline and learning. As a child Jones had conceived (even before he had the words for it) of truth as something buried deep, concealed, often hidden even from the self. In a letter to Mitchell, he cited the literary greatness of "the lonely ones," of the greatest artists—"Tolstoy, Wolfe, Dostiveski [*sic*], O'Neal [*sic*]"—and identified the source of their greatness as the closeness to the truth. "I think they live," he wrote, "because they have come up against the last veil between themselves and reality: Themselves."[25] Reality (truth) is, therefore, mysterious. To search for it is to try to solve a mystery. If this is so, if the truth of every individual is a mystery, then all humans share that much. There is, at the heart of things, a universal equality. And it is in that sense that the self can come to understand other selves. As Jones put it in his *Paris Review* interview: "You must really want to tell the truth about yourself (and no matter what any writer says, every character he creates is a part of himself, romanticized or unromanticized), but in order to do this you have to get down into yourself and try to find out what it is that makes us desire certain things and be afraid of certain other things." In that same interview he says he is pleased with the character of Dave Hirsh in *Some Came Running*: "Largely because my study of Dave Hirsh reaches much deeper levels, gets down much closer to that self-delusive deviousness we humans all labor under."[26]

  . . . that self-delusive deviousness we humans all labor under.

Two or three pertinent things, ones which affect his art, emerge from this assumption. One is a partial indifference to surfaces in his fiction. Jones was wonderfully sensitive to the rich texture of (superficial) experience, a man of five lively senses. He was, as both Willie Morris and James R. Giles noted, a man of keen *aesthetic* sensibility, and loved and appreciated painting and sculpture and good music, from the jazz of Oren Thaddeus (Hot Lips) Page and Sidney Bechet and Django Reinhardt to the music of Stravinsky and especially of Mozart. And he loved the good *things* of the world and spent much money, when he had it, on beautiful things. Finally, he had an extraordinary memory and was able to summon up past events and experiences in really astonishing detail. And yet because in his fiction the search for the truth, primarily the truth of character, would always be primary, the surfaces, while always adequate and often adroitly evocative, have been briskly applied like coats of paint. The aesthetic experience was always subordinate to inner dramatization.

Another result of his childhood's intuitive vision of the world was, inevitably, a great curiosity about other people. As he matured, this curiosity manifested itself as an interest and a sympathy which other people felt and were moved by.

Poet and novelist David Slavitt quit *Newsweek* in the late 1960s and wrote a couple of hugely successful best-sellers under the pseudonym "Henry Sutton." He and Jones had met on the *France*, crossing from the United States. "He was gracious and friendly," Slavitt writes, "and he invited us to call on him in Paris." His comments about Jones's sympathetic understanding are relevant:

> Jones had been up and down, and if you remember, I was in some ways an affront, a challenge, or pain in the ass back then. My success was noisy, and in some ways contemptuous. There are a lot of people who resented it, or resented my style of wearing it. He was, as I've said, generous. He was pleased that a good thing had happened to a young writer. He may have been a little rueful, or a little more shrewd than I gave him credit for, knowing how fickle the bitch goddess is and what I could surely expect in a few years. . . . His own experience had been mercurial. But he was cordial, welcoming, fun.[27]

At about that same time Jones told a reporter in Paris: "It is proper for a novelist to play different roles with different people to get attention and affection in a book. But it isn't proper in real life to make promises which deep in your heart you know you can't keep."[28] The reporter also made note of Jones's reaction to a plaque on the wall at 10, Rue des Deux Ponts, not far from Jones's Paris apartment: "To the memory of the 112 tenants of this house, of whom 40 were small children, [who were] deported in 1942 and died in German prison camps." Jones's remarks extend his sense of sympathy, which he had learned by hard knocks as a boy, to the social and political world:

> I make a point of reading the tablet every day. Depressing, but good for the soul. It symbolizes Civilization gone berserk. When a government has so much importance and power in the lives of men, it takes only one little thing to turn it backward to a previously unimagined barbarism. The terrifying thing is that it can happen any time in any country in the guise of morality.[29]

Another hard truth. The holocaust was seen less as an aberration, involving one people and one kind of government at one time in history, than as something that can happen any time in any country.

For the child within Jones to give way to the man, for inner rage and frustration to be converted into creative energy, he would have to experience and endure many things. And the experience of writing itself would also be his teacher. In a public panel discussion, "Creativity & Mental Health," he was asked, "What was your rage about before you sublimated it?"

"You name it," Jones answered. "Human corruption, human hypocrisy, human lying, human malice. Of which there is a great deal."[30]

And later, in the same discussion, he allowed that much of his anger and inner confusion had left him. "I can only conclude in general," he said, "the very act and process of writing was some kind of release of neuroses in myself. That slowly I was able to release this pressure and get rid of it in a way that almost now at the age of fifty-four has almost made me serene. Not quite, but nearly."[31]

But before the writing came the Army and the war.

In 1939 Jones graduated from Robinson High School (still standing and still used as a high school), and, unable to continue his education or to find a good job, he enlisted in the Army. He was never to see his mother or his father again. In less than three years both were dead. But on November 10, his father gave him three dollars, and they saw him off on a train. As soon as the train pulled out of sight of his waving parents and the station, he sat down with other recruits and got into a game of blackjack. He promptly won seven dollars more (a good omen), a not inconsiderable sum in those days when a soldier was paid $21 a month. (Jones was a lucky man with cards and would be for the rest of his life.) On that train ride to Fort Slocum, New York (on David's Island, in Long Island Sound near New Rochelle), Jones and the others evidently spent a day, or part of one, at liberty in New York City, seeing at least some of the sights. He made, and mailed home on December 5, an Empire State Observatory Voice Record and an autographed picture of Jack Dempsey. Three days later he sent a postcard of a mess hall at Fort Slocum, a place where, he said with all of a three-day veteran's assurance, "they herd you like cattle, work you like horses, and feed you like hogs."[32]

By early 1940 Jones had shipped out and was writing to Jeff from

Hickham Field in the Territory of Hawaii. There he was temporarily assigned to an MP outfit and wrote Jeff about the field uniform he wore—khaki pants, olive drab wool shirt, campaign hat, pistol, and three clips of ammunition—and how with that pistol on his hip, his campaign hat cocked, and with a freshly rolled cigarette he could "feel just like Gary Cooper."[33] He explained that the way to save money was to buy a big can of Union Leader tobacco for 70¢, cigarette papers for 5¢ per book, and a carton of matches for a dime. He was hoping to be permanently assigned to the Military Police. Meantime he wanted to borrow a little money to get some civilian clothes for off-duty hours. He was not much impressed by Waikiki Beach, but he loved the grandly elegant, pink stucco six-story Royal Hawaiian Hotel overlooking the beach from Honolulu's Kalukua Avenue, where, in those days, a single room with three meals cost $10 a day. Jones couldn't afford a room, but sometimes with a couple of dollars in his pocket he could go to the bar and drink like a tourist and a gentleman. More often he went to the Army-Navy YMCA on Hotel Street, where he worked on his diving and weight lifting and took instruction in boxing. He was learning that he was quick and well-coordinated, more of an athlete than he had guessed in his school days when he had made vain efforts to participate in team sports. Apparently he had done some boxing in high school. Small, quick, aggressive, and strong, he was a natural welterweight, and as he began to fill out and mature, he certainly *looked* like a fighter. He wrote well about fighting and sometimes referred to the irrepressible apprehension while waiting to go into the ring. It seems clear that he learned the one great lesson that fighting can teach. Joe Brown, a professional heavyweight of the 1930s, later boxing coach (and professor of art) at Princeton, used to put it this way: "The manly art of self-defense isn't manly, isn't an art, and is a lousy form of self-defense. But there is one good lesson you can learn from boxing. To win you've got to hit the other guy. And to hit the other guy you've got to get close enough so he can hit you."[34] No other way, no free lunch on either side. It is clear enough that Jones took this as plain truth. And it helps to explain his later bafflement at critics who felt they could throw brickbats at him and his work without any "hard feelings," and his bewilderment at the intellectuals of the 1960s who hoped to destabilize governments without getting their heads cracked.

Jones continued to read, avidly and unsystematically, and occasionally wrote a poem or a story. Later he would write Burroughs Mitchell that it was the example of Jeff, who had long been interested in writing, that inspired and encouraged him to write even before he had joined the Army.[35] One of the earliest surviving examples of his juvenilia is the poem "The King's Jester II," accompanying a letter to Jeff of May 22, 1940, with a reaction to the news of the war in Europe (in Belgium, the Netherlands, and France that month, as Germany invaded and drove the Allies toward the sea) and the sense that war was coming:

> We're young and we're strong,
> Our lives but begun,
> But we're ready to risk it and go,
> Just for the thrill and throw
> Our lives away 'gainst the foe.

As summer passed, the fear of war seems to have faded; for by August 21, 1940, he was thinking, once his enlistment had run out, of buying a motorcycle and going to South America.

By that time he had also transferred into the Infantry and was assigned to F Company, 2nd Battalion, of the 27th Infantry ("Wolfhound") Regiment, stationed at D Quad in Schofield Barracks. He began to write his letters on Wolfhound stationery with the wolf's head badge and the Latin motto, *Nec Aspera Terrent* (literally "Not Even Difficulties Frighten Them") boldly printed on it. In the United States, Selective Service had begun, but this was a proud Regular Army outfit, organized in 1901 and active ever since, fighting in the Philippine Insurrection and later in Siberia in 1918 and 1919. It had been assigned as part of the old Hawaiian Division on March 1, 1921, with headquarters at Schofield Barracks. On August 26, 1941, the Hawaiian Division became the 25th. In the South Pacific it would earn its nickname, "Tropic Lightning." But in those peacetime days the Regular Army was primarily regimental. Except in combat, the division was conceived of as an administrative unit. You joined and served with a regiment. Jones was eager to begin his infantry training, but he told Jeff that he did not want people in this outfit to know that he had done any boxing. He said that he would not box if they did find out and asked him to.

At this point we move into the world which would become *From Here to Eternity.*

In uniform as M.P., Hickman Field, Hawaii, 1940

OPPOSITE : *Working at his father's desk*

Schofield Barracks, Company F, 27th Infantry, November 1941
(Jones in second row, fourth from right)

The peacetime Army was bugle calls, reveille to taps, close order drill, spit and polish, discipline, road marches, rudimentary weapons training, barracks life, not much money, and plenty of time, time on your hands. It was hard to make the infantry into much more than a half-day job. Schofield Barracks, a permanent barracks still in use today, sat out among pineapple fields, north of Honolulu on Route 99, with the dark shapes of the Waianae Range of mountains rising to the west. Writing in *Viet Journal*, Jones remarked that "Schofield Barracks is probably the most beautiful post the U.S. Army has, or ever had." But he had not noticed the beauty of its situation then. He performed his duties (soon serving as a company clerk) and, when he was allowed and could afford it, boarded a bus and went downtown to the Hotel Street area—to the Army-Navy Y; to Wu Fat's Chinese Restaurant, to the seedy wonders of the New Senator Hotel. Here is how he recalls it in *Viet Journal*:

> The area had once been a swarming hive of bars, street vendors, tattoo parlors, shooting galleries, photo galleries, market shops, fruit and vegetable shops, and hooker joints occupying the rooms upstairs and the labeled hotels. . . . Once it had been our Mecca, toward which we rose and prayed every morning, before Reveille. Compressed into a half-mile area down by the docks between the King's Palace and the little river, and bursting at the seams to break out, it had been the bottomless receptacle of our dreams and frustrations, and of our money. The payday payroll.[36]

Other times, if he had just enough money for it, he would go to the post theater and see a movie. Otherwise he was off alone to the post library, where he happened on Thomas Wolfe's *Look Homeward, Angel*. He was deeply moved; it inspired and soon confirmed in him the dream of being a writer. In a letter to Jeff he called Wolfe the "greatest writer that has lived, Shakespeare included."[37] That first passionate impression would be modified and qualified in later years; yet he was always loyal to (and grateful for) Wolfe's influence on his life and art.

Perhaps the most thorough statement by Jones of what he was reading at the time is to be found in his contribution to *Attacks of Taste* (1971). His statement is, as one comes to expect from Jones, very matter-of-fact and straightforward:

My serious reading only began at the age of eighteen, after graduation from high school and while I was an enlisted man in the regular army. This was occasioned by my reading of Thomas Wolfe, followed by Joyce, Hemingway, Faulkner. From these I went into a thorough study of late nineteenth century and early twentieth century English novelists, such as Conrad, Arnold Bennet[t], Aldous Huxley, Galsworthy etc. By this time I was nineteen, almost twenty, and a part-time student at the University of Hawaii. Of these I guess my favorite for quite awhile [*sic*] was Wolfe's *Look Homeward Angel*, largely because it was such a marvelous portrait of an adolescent teenage American boy, and I would recommend it to all people; after that, just about everything of Conrad and Galsworthy's *The Forsyte Saga*. It was only later that I came to appreciate, more, Joyce and Faulkner.[38]

Jones's wife says that throughout their lives together Jones read constantly, that he could thrive on very little sleep and that long after others were asleep he would be reading into the early hours. Orders and receipts, among the papers at the Beinecke and The Humanities Research Center, covering the years he lived in the United States show a constant flow of books of all kinds going to Jones from Scribner's, from Brentano's, from bookstores in Cincinnati, St. Louis, Chicago. And after the money from *From Here to Eternity* began to come in, he spent generously on rare books and first editions to build up his library.

The peacetime Army taught Jones much about life and about the lives of others very different from himself. But it also worked to convert his inner, often stifled rage into creative energy. For in order to survive in the Army he had to learn new dimensions of guile and self-control. As an enlisted man he had to learn to be anonymous, often almost as invisible as Ralph Ellison's Invisible Man. He learned to carry his precious, secret inner life like water in cupped hands. Thus, in that sense, the Army did for him what it is supposed to—it made a man of him.

In his eulogy for James Jones, published in the *New York Times Book Review*, Irwin Shaw described the old Army Jones was part of: "It was a world of outcasts from American society, a world of rejected and savage men for whom the only honors they could hope for had to come from their fellow troopers—for excellence in the field, for individual toughness, by inspiring fear or by a sly outwitting of authority."[39] Shaw's picture is partly true, but needs to be qualified; for it has been influenced more by the power of fiction, *From Here to Eternity*, than by fact. In actuality it was not easy to gain access to a job in the peacetime Army, during the Depression. Jones was, in fact, lucky to find a place in the Army when he did. By and large, the enlisted men of the Army in those days were not "outcasts" or "rejected and savage men." Rather it was those people, the special and different ones—Prewitt and Maggio and Stark and Warden and Malloy—who fascinated the young Jones most because they were exotics in uniform. And the uniform helped disguise the truth of them. A perhaps more accurate estimate is offered by Pearl K. Bell in "The Wars of James Jones," where she sees the Army as the *whole* of American society. "Indeed the army was the world," she writes, "the great American cross-section of rubes and city-slickers, leaders and lackeys, bullies and men of honor, fags and he-men, pillars of society and Dead End kids, redneck louts and visionary rebels."[40] More inclusive and more simple is the statement by Joan Didion that "Jones had known a great simple truth: the Army was nothing more or less than life itself."[41]

There was an old tradition, as old as this nation, and still well-preserved in the midwestern heartlands and in the South when Jones came along, of (younger sons especially) going to the military as a profession, or at least (as Melville had gone to sea) as an education. Part of that education was a matter of pride. You wanted to serve in a combat branch if possible—infantry, cavalry (armor), artillery. There was something mildly shameful and distinctly second-rate about the other supporting branches. Jones had been worried about his father's reaction to his transfer into the infantry. He need not have been so. On New Year's Eve of 1940 Dr. Jones wrote to his son about it: "I'm glad you like it so much better in the infantry, Jim. It really is the backbone of any army, and you get more experience there than in any other branch."[42] And another old tradition was a democratic one, which viewed service in the ranks as appropriate for everyone, *especially* for future officers. For who could command free men who had not served in the ranks first? For all its injustice and, judged by hindsight, brutality, the American Army was unique; for, unlike the armies of other countries, the caste and class system in ours was not an exact reflection, not a precise continuation of the social hierarchy of society. Thus, in one sense, the tensions between officers and enlisted men were greater, since almost every American soldier felt himself to be the equal of any officer in every way except for the badges of privilege and authority. Most American soldiers felt they could do a better job all around than the officers who commanded them. In World War II this self-confidence proved to be one of the great and secret strengths of the U.S. Army. In other armies, even among the skilled, courageous, and feared Germans, when the officers were killed the unit usually disintegrated. The American Army seemed to have an inexhaustible resource of potential leaders. Jones reflected the typical American attitude toward officers, even on occasion chiding his friend and editor, Burroughs Mitchell, for having been one. For example, in a letter concerned with cuts of four-letter words which Mitchell was proposing, Jones wrote: "I don't know if I can make you understand. You think I put those things in arbitrarily, just for simple shock value. But it isn't that. You see, you were an officer. Officers are inclined to be a little more polite about such things."[43] Moreover, in a section of *WWII*, "Is History Written by the Upper Classes for the Upper Classes," Jones makes a strong argument for the existence of an American class system. "As in most wars," he writes, "in the United States in World War II (and I assume in most of the nations) most of the commanding was done by the upper classes, and most of the fighting was done by the lower."[44] It is, of course, a very vague class system he's using, musing on. Missing is the enormous middle class, which made up the bulk of America's fighting forces, in peace and in war, up through the Korean War—and which included James Jones. As I *interpret* his point, in this crucial little chapter of *WWII*, it is less about sociopolitical systems than he may have thought and much more about something else that concerned him deeply —the truth. It is about the failure of imagination on the part of intellectuals who, as it happens, are either from or are educated into the "upper classes" and who lose contact with and concern for those who labor and fight for them. Their histories are therefore suspect insofar as they are removed from the textures of quotidian reality.

In any case Jones's attitude has been slightly misinterpreted by some Marxist-oriented critics as neatly exemplary of the class struggle between the *proletariat* and the *bourgeoisie*. This perhaps explains why leftist critics have admired the military novels of Jones and usually panned his novels dealing with civilian life. For Jones finds civilian life, American society, and the American psyche more complex and ambiguous than these critics might have preferred. People interested primarily in a literature that depicts and promotes the venerably Victorian concept of *class struggle* are likely to look askance at a point of view that does not allow for the easy definition and recognition of good guys and bad guys. It was part of Jones's credo as an artist not to think in those terms. As he wrote to Burroughs Mitchell in 1949, "As long as you can be everybody (without feeling ashamed) you are a real writer. When you start dividing them up into Heroes and Villains you're done."[45]

Jones's viewpoint is deeply rooted in the American populist tradition, something which plagued our armed forces from the days of the colonial militia through the Civil War (when rich men, north and south, were permitted to evade serving in the army) until finally, as a result of the college-deferment policies of Selective Service, in Vietnam the Army began to take on a classically proletariat character. World War II, the rush to put millions of men in arms, was the beginning of the change. But it should be understood that Jones's reluctance to be an officer, to go to OCS, was, at the time, correct and conventional, *traditional.* Here is another example of the old America and the new. In Eastern urban centers the children and grandchildren of immigrants from Europe, especially the Mediterranean and Eastern Europe, one of whose primary motivations in coming to America had been to avoid involuntary military service, could not conceive of anyone joining the service voluntarily without being, in one sense or another, a social outcast. The triumph of the new America over the old, including the *changes* that have accompanied it and, a later sequence of unpopular wars, have reinforced that bias against the military life. But James Jones, the novelist, was able to make myth outweigh fact; for by his focused concentration on rare individuals, the genuine rebels at the center of *From Here to Eternity,* he has prevented us from seeing just how basically dull and inveterately middle-class the American Army really was until the war changed everything.

While the young Jones was serving out his hitch in the Army on Oahu, thousands of miles from kin and home, he was dealt two traumatic blows. Among the papers at the Humanities Research Center is an envelope postmarked Robinson; and it bears, pathetically in his father's handwriting, the words "Bad News" on the front. Inside his father explains that he wanted to give Jones some sort of warning before he eagerly ripped open the letter for news from home. The letter tells him (and there is another letter from Jeff as well) that his mother is dead: "She died last night about 8 o'clock, after everything the doctors and attention could do to prevent it."[46] Thus Jones never had a chance to make peace or come to terms with the image of his mother that had haunted his childhood. She was taken from him before he had a chance to know her, perhaps to forgive her (and himself) if not to love her. Ada Blessing Jones was a diabetic who had become a Christian Scientist in her search for some kind of religious fulfillment. She died, apparently, of complications brought about by her diabetes; but the immediate cause of death was congestive heart failure, the same thing that would kill Jones in middle age.

It does not require a Freudian psychiatrist to see that Jones's relationships with women would be made even more complex as a result of his mother's early death, or that he would have to work through intense and ambiguous relationships with older women, especially with Lowney Handy, before he finally met and married Gloria Mosolino. He was aware of this problem himself very early. And he made a note, on October 23, 1942, in a small black notebook he carried in those days. (Taped on it, evidently in case he should be killed or wounded in combat was: "Send to: Jeff Jones/307 W. Lincoln/Findlay, Ohio.") "I've only found three women—who were not sluts," he wrote to himself (and posterity), "who feel about sex as I do. They were quite a bit older than me, & I think only one of them was really honest."[47]

In March 1942, after the overwhelming national trauma of Pearl Harbor had plunged the country into war, Dr. Ramon Jones killed himself. Dr. Jones, who had served in World War I, spent February of 1942 trying to reenlist. On February 25, 1942, he had sent a letter, vaguely addressed to "Commanding Officer/Illinois Military Area" pleading for a chance. "My physical condition is excellent, and all I ask is a chance."[48] The Army did nothing to encourage Dr. Jones in his hopes. He shot himself. As the *Robinson Daily News* described it (on page 1 of the Thursday, March 12, 1942, issue) :

Dr. Jones was apparently seated in a rocking chair in the back room of his office when he fired the automatic into the back of his head. The first shell misfired, and was ejected, being found lying in front of the chair on the floor. He apparently laid [*sic*] in the chair for sometime, indicated by his blood soaked coat on the back of the chair. It was then thought that he regained consciousness to take a handkerchief from his pocket, which was found in his hand, before he fell forward to the floor and attempted to make his way to a couch on the other side of the office. His body was found beside the couch.

Several people had seen Dr. Jones on the morning of the eleventh, but he was apparently drunk or, as the *Robinson Argus* put it in its March 19 account, "not in condition to do business." The *Argus* described the discovery of the body in the afternoon of the eleventh:

> Dr. Jones, 55 years of age, was found lying on the floor in a back room of his offices over the Oakley-Kroger store on the south side of the square shortly after 4:30 o'clock Wednesday afternoon by his daughter, Mary Ann, 17, who had just come from high school.[49]

On March 22, Jones wrote Mary Ann (Tink) a letter, telling her that he had had a premonition about "Dad's death."[50] He urged her not to blame their father, for it was not his fault that he was weak. After that, Jones had to live with the fact of his father's suicide. One strategy he seems to have hit upon was to be entirely open and straightforward about it. He referred to it, off and on over the years, in letters and interviews, as one might refer to a handicap, a chronic physical disability. Over the years the edge of bitterness was dulled. In 1948 he referred to it in a letter to Burroughs Mitchell, saying, "Maybe I'll end up an ironist like Swift and hate everybody, to keep from sentimentally shooting myself like the old man did."[51] A 1950 letter to Mitchell adds the detail that a newspaper man "took a number of photographs of my father as he lay on the floor of his office after having shot himself in the head in a fit of drunken self-pity."[52] But, unlike some fellow writers (Hemingway and John Berryman, for example), who had to face the same terrible event in their lives and were fatally hurt by it, Jones lived long enough to make a peace with his father's ghost. His last word on the subject is on the first page of *Viet Journal*.

> Advancing middle age does strange things to men. In January of 1942 my father went around to the nearest recruiting station and tried to volunteer for a commission in the Infantry, as a lieutenant. He was 56 at the time, a known alcoholic, a mediocre vet of World War I, and a failure at his profession of dentist. The Army turned him down. Cold. They didn't even want him as a dentist. He wrote me a rather de-

spairing letter about it. I read it, wondering how he could imagine the Army would want him for anything. At the time I was on a beach position in Honolulu, a corporal of Infantry myself. Before that spring was out, my father was to commit suicide by shooting himself in the head. Later I would speculate often whether that turndown by the Army had not been such a slap in the face that it helped awaken him to what he was, what he had become, and he could not stand to face it. I loved my father, and I hated to see it end like that. He deserved a better fate.[53]

What was left of the family by spring of 1942? Jones's brother Jeff and his sister—and Uncle Charles with whom they had never really gotten along. And there was Aunt Mollie, his mother's sister, out in California. Aunt Mollie had always written to him, sent him cards and presents, and throughout the war regularly sent Jones letters, often V-mail, (overseas correspondence on microfilm, to save shipping space), most of which he kept. It was Aunt Mollie to whom he wrote in 1948 when Edward Weeks accepted Jones's first story, "Temper of Steel," for *Atlantic*. "You hoped to be here," Jones wrote her, "to still be living, you said, when I made the grade. Well, this is it. This is the first published work I've had."[54] Aunt Mollie lived on a good while longer, to the age of 104.[55]

Between the death of his mother and his father's suicide came the Japanese attack on Pearl Harbor. This would become the climax of *From Here to Eternity*, the scene he was proudest of. (Ironically it was rejected by Weeks for the *Atlantic*.) Jones also wrote about it, more personally, in *WWII*. He was on duty that Sunday, as guard orderly for the colonel (usually a merely ceremonial job) and was having his Sunday breakfast in the mess hall. Breakfast was on his mind—"a bonus ration of a half-pint of milk, to go with your eggs and pancakes and syrup, also Sunday specials." They listened to the sounds of explosions from Wheeler Field (where he would have been, most likely, if he had not transferred to infantry), but thought nothing of it. "It was not til the first low-flying fighter came skidding, whammering low overhead with his MG's going that we ran outside, still clutching our half-pints of milk to keep them from being stolen, aware with a sudden sense of awe that we were seeing and acting in a genuine moment of history." In *WWII* Jones describes standing outside and watching a Japanese plane fly so low and close that he could see the pilot's grin and his hachimaki, "the headband worn by medieval samurai when going into battle, usually with some religious slogan of Shinto or Emperor worship inked on it."[56] Like Pfc. Richard Mast, the protagonist of *The Pistol*, Jones spent that morning as a runner, carrying messages to and from Regimental Headquarters. Later that day, F Company, together with the rest of the outfit, moved out in truck convoy to take up and prepare beach defense positions at windy Makapuu Head, six miles from the company's command post at Hanauma Bay. They were to guard against any possible invasion landing, which in those panicky early days seemed distinctly possible.

Company F hurriedly made five pillboxes, carved out of the rock with heavy gasoline-driven Barco drills (which gave Jones occasional trouble with numbness in his hands for the rest of his life) for their water-cooled caliber .30 machine guns. They dug in, laid barbed wire on the beach, stood guard duty, and waited. And waited. From that moment on his letters home were censored. Those which have survived have the censors' numbers (sometimes a signature) on them, and occasionally there are blacked out or razored out words or sections.

In those early months of the war, combat for Americans in the Pacific meant the Philippines until they fell and the big air and sea battles of Java Sea, Coral Sea, and Midway. Sailors and pilots from the victory at Midway —where the Japanese advance was finally halted—came and went in Hawaii. And Jones's outfit received a bronze battle star for Midway "to go with the orange, red-striped Asiatic-Pacific Campaign medal and ribbon," chiefly because of "some geographical technicality."[57] Jones remained at the beach position for months; then in September, the unit was relieved and pulled back to Schofield Barracks again for a period of combat training, which Jones has described in *WWII* as being "woefully inadequate, and we knew it."[58] In the midst of all this he somehow found time to enroll in two courses—Creative Writing and British Masterpieces—at the University of Hawaii, courses meeting on Monday, Wednesday and Friday for five academic credits. Three teachers at the University took a serious interest in him and his work—Gaylord C. Leroy, Carl Stroven, and Laura Schwartz. He wrote poems and stories. A number of poems from that period are among the papers at the Beinecke, for example "The Goon Walking" and "Hilltop Reverie," the latter of which would be incorporated into *The Pistol*. He also seems to have planned and have done some work on a novel entitled "Black Laughter." When he shipped out later, his manuscripts were stored and kept for him by Dr. Leroy, whose wife told

Jones that one day he would be "in a class with Steinbeck and Wolfe."[59] He would not recover those early manuscripts until 1946 when he was already working on *From Here to Eternity*. While attending classes at the University he also met a young woman, Peggy Carson, whom he mentioned in a letter to Jeff as someone he might want to marry.[60] After he shipped out, he wrote to her, and he continued to correspond with her until 1953. There are also letters from this period to Virginia Moore and to a cheerful girl from Robinson, Barbara Van Dusen, who always called him by his old nickname "Jeeper" and seems to have been more a buddy, a pen pal, than a romantic interest. There are a number of tantalizing references to "Mary the Waheni" in his letters to Jeff. But there are also cautionary comments not to believe anything he says about successes with women.

Abruptly, in November, the training schedule at Schofield was canceled. The Wolfhound Regiment packed up and prepared to ship out. They guessed for Australia. Jones could not know this, but the 25th Division, commanded by Major General J. Lawton (Lightning Joe) Collins, had been officially alerted to prepare to leave Oahu on October 19 and was going to Guadalcanal in the Solomon Islands to relieve the Marines there. Soldiers of the America L Division, composed mostly of activated National Guard regiments, including the 132nd Infantry of the Illinois National Guard, had already been arriving there in stages since early November. The 25th Division shipped out in stages also. In a diary he was trying to keep (this is the last entry until sometime in February) Jones noted that his troopship sailed at 1:00 P.M. on December 6, 1942.[61]

He was headed for the first major counteroffensive campaign conducted by American forces in the South Pacific. The First Marine Division had landed at Guadalcanal on August 7, 1942, taking and then holding and extending the small airfield on the north side of the island near Lunga Point. Both the Japanese and the Americans had poured men and material resources into the battle for control of the island. Beginning with the August 9 disaster named the Battle of Savo Island, there had been five full-scale naval surface battles, at night, in view of the shores of Guadalcanal, with the loss of many ships and men on both sides. There were far more casualties in the Navy than in the ground forces. And there had been innumerable air raids and air battles with heavy losses, though the Japanese losses in planes and particularly in skilled pilots were much higher. After the war Captain Tashikazu Ohmae, chief of staff for the Japanese Southeastern Fleet, described that loss as crucial to the Japanese defeat:

Aunt Mollie and Mary Ann, 1952

Keir Dullea in The Thin Red Line

"First we lost our best carriers at Midway, then our pilots in the Solomons."[62] But for James Jones, as for thousands of other American G.I.'s and their Japanese enemies, these grand strategic considerations meant next to nothing. They would have to settle things in brutal ground combat, carried on at close quarters in an inhospitable climate and on extremely difficult terrain. In *WWII* Jones argued that "the whole history of my generation's World War II has been written, not wrongly so much, but in a way that gave precedence to the viewpoints of strategists, tacticians and theorists, but gave little more than lip service to the viewpoint of the hairy, swiftly aging, fighting lower class soldier."[63] Jones's remedy for that failure would be his fiction. The experiences of the peacetime Army, up to and including Pearl Harbor, went into *From Here to Eternity*; the months at the Makapuu Head beach position became the essence of *The Pistol*, as well as of the story "The Way It Is," first published in *Harper's* in June 1949, and the days and nights of F Company, 27th Infantry (fictionalized as Charlie Company), became *The Thin Red Line*. From both personal and official histories of the campaign, taken together with Jones's comments and memories, in letters and interviews as well as published work, it is clear that while his artistic *selectivity*, among people, places, and the events he witnessed with F Company, is strictly controlled, he neither invented nor distorted much of the experience for that novel. Both in general and in details, its closeness to the reality of the experience makes it not unlike a documentary film in which the creator's task has been mostly a matter (subtle and complex as that may be) of editing the material. Which seems to be more or less what Jones had in mind. In a notebook from the early 1950s Jones makes this note about "the combat novel," which he had been considering as a serious project since at least 1946: "I want to make it as 'photographic'—but good and bad—as all the so-called 'photographic news' accounts written in detail. But I would also like to achieve a 'photographicness' of both inside and outside, as starkly objective and without literary embellishments as possible."[64]

A great many books have been written which deal with aspects of the Guadalcanal campaign, some by distinguished writers (William Manchester, Richard Tregaskis, Samuel Eliot Morison). But the two finest are Jones's *The Thin Red Line* and the nonfiction book *Into the Valley: A Skirmish of the Marines*, by John Hersey (1943), which like *The Thin Red Line* dealt with a single company action, during the Third Battle of the

Matanikau River that took place well before the 27th Infantry arrived. It is clear from both books that all of it was tough going, that every foot of territory had to be bought and paid for the hard way. There is a deep difference, however. Hersey was there as a visitor, a kind of daring tourist, a reporter for *Time*. Jones was there, with the rest of the G.I.s, for the duration, or until they carried him out feet first. . . .

It appears that Jones and F Company went ashore at Guadalcanal on or about New Year's Day, 1943 (certainly no later than January 4), with the rest of Colonel William A. McCulloch's Wolfhound Regiment. By then the last of the First Marine Division, "the raggedy-ass marines," who had suffered 2,736 casualties and 75 percent of whom were estimated to be suffering from malaria (the *average* Marine lost between twenty and thirty pounds during the campaign) had already shipped out. Elements of the 2nd Marines, together with the Americal Division, and the 25th, all under the command of Major General Alexander Patch, were to pick up the fight where the Marines had left off. From off the beach, with its remnant of blasted and battered coconut palms left over from the prewar copra plantations, F Company moved inland into a strange and different landscape. To the south, thirty miles away at the island's widest point, was a range of mountains eight thousand feet high. Between shore and mountains lay ridges, plains covered with tough kunai grass and dense tropical rain forest. Movement of supplies and equipment was extremely difficult. Movement by troops was trouble enough, and all accounts, including Jones's, make a good deal out of the terrible problems of moving the wounded from the front to the aid stations and field hospitals. (Helicopter ambulances still lay in the future.) The rain forest jungle was dark and steamy, overgrown, perfect for camouflaged snipers in trees. The plains and ridges were perfect terrain for mortar fire—at which the Japanese were past masters.

Intelligence, for both sides, was at best rudimentary and most often faulty. So there was no way that the Americans could have known that they were up against an enemy who no longer had any artillery to speak of and no hope of air support, an enemy sick with malaria and other tropical diseases, an enemy who was literally starving to death. Nor could they or their leaders have known that at the highest level the Japanese had only just then (and finally) given up all hope of holding or retaking Guadalcanal. The Japanese would soon execute a brilliant and courageous evacuation, saving thousands of their soldiers from death or capture. But in early

January, as the 27th prepared to go into action, the Americans were going up against a bitterly determined rearguard action, fighting on the enemy's turf and on the enemy's terms. Using snipers, wonderfully accurate mortar fire, and carefully concealed, dug-in machine guns, and firing emplacements covering fields of fire of known ranges, the Japanese could do a lot with a little. Though they did not know this, the Americans would not have to contend against the mass counterattacks, which we named banzai charges. The Japanese had employed these as a tactic earlier, though not since the Sendai Division was shattered in its attempt to overrun Bloody Ridge and retake Henderson Field in late October. Still, the Japanese, half out of pride and half out of fear of what would happen if they surrendered, would stand and die. Like the Marines, they chose death before dishonor.

On January 8, General Collins issued his Field Order No. 1, which called for the 27th Infantry to take a 900-foot-high hill mass, a system of ridges called the Galloping Horse ("The Elephant's Head" in *The Thin Red Line*) because of its appearance in aerial photographs.

As detailed in *The Thin Red Line*, the route march from the bivouac area to the front proved exhausting for the troops and would later lead to serious supply shortages. As described by John Miller, Jr. in *Guadalcanal: The First Offensive*: "Rough ground and insufficient motor transport complicated the movement of weapons, spare parts, ammunition and water. . . ."[65] The water shortage was to prove serious, almost disastrous; for throughout the campaign dehydration and heat exhaustion put as many men out of action as the enemy did. On January 10, 1st Battalion and 3rd Battalion went into action, with 2nd Battalion (including F Company and Corporal James Jones) in reserve. Second Battalion held a position on a forward slope with a good overview of the action, which began at 0635 with a time-on-target artillery barrage fired by the 25th Division Artillery and by the 75mm Pack Howitzers of the 2nd Battalion, 10th Marines and the 155mm howitzers of the America's 221st Field Artillery Battalion. Time-on-target fire is prearranged so that the first rounds, coming from a variety of weapons at various and different locations, will all arrive on target and explode simultaneously. "This time-on-target (TOT) 'shoot' was the first divisional firing of the Guadalcanal campaign," Miller writes, "and may have been the first divisional TOT fired by American artillerymen in World War II."[66]

James Jones witnessed all of this. More to the point, he found ways to use every detail later in his fiction. From Jones's point of view the ridges of the Galloping Horse erupted with explosions precisely at 0635 and continued to do so for the next thirty minutes as 5,700 rounds were fired. After that came an air attack. Twelve P-39's and twelve dive bombers dropped 500-pound demolition bombs and 325-pound depth charges on enemy positions. After which L and I companies of the 3rd Battalion, with K in reserve, attacked Hill 52-53. The 3rd had a bad day of it, took heavy casualties, and due to mistakes of various kinds, was unsuccessful in accomplishing its mission. Miller describes a typical error of this first day: "Captain Rohot (C.O. of 'L' Company) ordered the platoon to withdraw 100 yards east to enable him to cover the whole crest (of Hill 50) with mortar fire. The message was relayed to the platoon leader, but, as the words '100 yards' had been inadvertently dropped from the message by the time he received it, he pulled his men all the way back to Hill 51."[67] Night found them about where they had started and much the worse for wear. It then fell to 2nd Battalion, with F Company on the left, to relieve 3rd Battalion the next morning. What followed was a difficult but successful attack, made more difficult, as in *The Thin Red Line*, by an acute shortage of drinking water on a couple of hot days. It turned out to be a crucial fight. As Samuel Griffith wrote of it in *The Battle for Guadalcanal* (1963): "On the following morning (January 11) the 2nd Battalion relieved the 3rd, and immediately attacked along a spiny, kunai-covered ridge toward a well-concealed and strongly held position on its southern tip, designated 'Hill 53.' The battalion could not know at the moment its companies jumped off that its lonely battle on this desolate ridge would bring merited distinction to itself, to the regiment, and the 25th Division."[68] It took a cloudburst to ease the water shortage and two more days to finish up the action, which included a daring assault on a Japanese machine-gun emplacement by volunteers from F Company led by the battalion executive officer, Captain Charles W. Davis. Miller's official Army history describes this event as follows:

The five men had crawled to within ten yards of the position when the Japanese hurled grenades at them. Although their aim was accurate, the grenades failed to explode. The Americans replied with eight grenades which did explode, then sprang up to rush the enemy, some of whom fled. Captain Davis' rifle jammed after one round. He threw it away, drew his pistol and the five men leaped among the surviving Japanese and finished them with rifles and pistols. . . . For his gallant action, Captain Davis received the Medal of Honor.[69]

This was one of the six Congressional Medals of Honor that would be awarded to members of the 25th Division in World War II. Neither the incident, nor the typical irony that the officer alone received the highest medal for a "gallant action," which had involved all five men, was lost on Jones. And these matters are to be found, in place and in sequence, in *The Thin Red Line*. But during those three days of action two things happened to James Jones which are not part of official published histories, though they marked his life forever and figure in the novel. First, Jones killed a Japanese soldier in hand-to-hand combat. At some point, early on in the action, he left the safety of his slit trench and went into the cover of some dense jungle and undergrowth to relieve himself. He had pulled down his pants and was squatting when out of the thick bushes came a scarecrow-ragged Japanese soldier who attacked him with a bayonet. Jones managed to defend himself, disarm the Jap, and kill him. As he told the story in later years to Gloria, and to some few close friends, he fought for his own life and killed his man, who proved to be half-starved and disease-ridden, probably half-crazed if the truth were known. From his wallet Jones said he took some photographs of the soldier in better days with his family and friends. And he swore he would not kill again. (There are several faded, wallet-size photographs of a Japanese soldier and his family and buddies in an envelope among the Jones papers at Texas.)

Jones's resolution was not to be immediately tested, because not long after that (on January 12), and before he had any serious opportunity to harm anyone else, he was hit by fragments of a mortar shell. It was a head wound, the messiest and most fearful kind. It smashed his glasses and made him believe he was close to death (as it does to Corporal Fife in *The Thin Red Line*). When the wound turns out to be superficial and not likely to keep him out of combat for long, Fife is at once furious and disappointed. We cannot know exactly what *Jones* felt, though we do have his description of the moment he was wounded in WWII.

I think I screamed, myself, when I was hit. I thought I could vaguely remember somebody yelling. I blacked out for several seconds, and had a dim impression of someone stumbling to his feet with his hands to his face. It wasn't me. Then I came to myself several yards down the slope, bleeding like a stuck pig and blood running all over my face. It must have been a dramatic scene. As soon as I found I wasn't dead or dying, I was pleased to get out of there as fast as I could.[70]

Apparently Jones had not troubled to notify the Army that his next of kin was dead, so that when he was wounded on Guadalcanal, a telegram of notification was sent to Dr. "Raymond" Jones on February 12, 1943, and listed as "delivered" at 8:00 A.M. on the thirteenth.

DEEPLY REGRET TO INFORM YOU REPORT FROM SOUTH PACIFIC AREA DATED FEBRUARY 9 STATES YOUR SON CORPORAL JAMES R. JONES WAS WOUNDED IN ACTION JANUARY 20 PERIOD REPORTS WILL BE FORWARDED WHEN RECEIVED

SIGNED
ULIO, THE ADJUTANT GENERAL[71]

So much for bureaucracy. They sent the telegram to a dead man, got his name wrong and the date that Jones was wounded wrong as well.

According to Jones in *WWII*, he spent a week in the hospital, then rejoined the outfit in time for the last part of the campaign—the taking of the village of Kokumbona on January 23. After that the 27th was pulled back close to Henderson Field for rest and because General Patch feared a major new Japanese assault on the island. But within a week the last Japanese had been evacuated from Guadalcanal. After a rest period, the 25th Division was to prepare to move on to the next action—which would prove to be New Georgia, also in the Solomons.

In the Beinecke Library there is a letter of January 28, 1943, from Jones to Jeff, his first chance to write since he went into combat. He tells the story of his wound, the hole in his helmet, and the destruction of his glasses. He talks about some of the things he had learned, what it all *meant* to him. The main thing he had learned was that there was nothing you could do or not do in combat to save your own life. Life or death was largely a matter of luck. He had a feeling that his luck had run out on him, that he was going to die.

He was wrong about his luck. Jones had a bad ankle, one which he had injured and reinjured and had to keep carefully taped to walk on at all. Thanks to his first sergeant and to a surgeon who believed an infantry man ought to be able to walk without pain and difficulty, Jones was shipped out to have an operation on his ankle. According to Willie Morris, he went first to a hospital at Efate in the New Hebrides, then to Auckland, New Zealand, where there are pleasant references in his letters to a nurse named Alma Schumaker from Anna, Illinois. By February 19, 1943, he was feeling somewhat better about himself and the future. He could not help beginning to make plans, to have hopes just in case he should survive the war. "I still don't expect to come out," he wrote Jeff, "but I'm not so bitter about it now."[72]

Not long after, he was on board the hospital ship *Matsonia* and headed for home—which is where *Whistle*, the final novel of the trilogy and Jones's last book, begins.

By May 22, 1943, he was at Letterman General Hospital in San Francisco and writing the news to Jeff and beginning to feel and express some of the shock he had on returning as a man to a world so different from the one he had left as a boy, a few short years before. True to itself, the Army dutifully notified Jeff (now next of kin) three weeks later (June 8, 1943) that Jones was coming back: "A REPORT DATED JUNE 5, 1943, HAS BEEN RECEIVED FROM THE PACIFIC AREA, STATING THAT YOUR BROTHER, CORPORAL JAMES JONES, 6, 915, 544 IS BEING RETURNED TO U.S."[73] It was sent to the wrong address, however, the old Findlay, Ohio, address—Jeff was now working for the American Red Cross in Miami.

By that time, James Jones was at Kennedy General Hospital in Memphis. All the extant documents and evidence from the period support the fictional picture Jones presents in *Whistle* or in his recollections in *WWII*—and in flashes in other pieces, for instance a scene of his going to the movies and laughing out loud at a war film, in "Phony War Films."[74] In his April 7, 1949, letter to Burroughs Mitchell, describing his "wild time" in Memphis, he said, "I had a two-room suite at the Peabody six weeks straight and loaned the key to anybody who wanted it when I couldn't get into town."[75] He may also have kept a room at the Hotel Claridge, for he had a lot of stationery from there which he used along with Red Cross writing paper for his correspondence and for poems and stories. He also wrote and kept notes in a notebook labeled "Day Book Belonging to Pvt.

Gordon G. Merritt, Service Co, 27th Inf."[76] (Its contents include many practice signatures of Jones's name, photos of a couple of girls, a brief story by Merritt—clearly in another hand than Jones's—called "The Story of Peter Pringle," and a great deal of miscellaneous material in Jones's hand, concerning a wounded soldier in a hospital, here named Weinerbaum General Hospital. It would be called Kilrainey Army General Hospital in *Whistle*.) There are, in the Beinecke, fragments of short stories from this period. There are poems he carefully copied out and evidently folded and kept handy—"Invictus," by William Ernest Henley, several short poems by Stephen Crane: "The Heart," "War Is Kind," "A Little Ink More or Less," "The Wayfarer," and "I Saw a Man." And there are many poems of his own, ranging from short, terse, ironic verses somewhat in the manner of Crane—"I Have a God" and "Hunger"—to longer, more complex, and personal poems with titles like "What Is Understanding?" "Fighter for Freedom," "Pain & a Dark Soul Growing," "Bloody Claws" ("Sitting alone—as always—& brooding in a bar . . ."), and "The White & the Black," which includes these lines:

> My gang, my friends, my fellow wolves &
>   drunkards
> Are cursing them, Democracy & Freedom,
> And are dying for them
> And the things they curse[77]

Or this, from an untitled poem, referring directly to the experience he wrote about twenty years later in "Phony War Films":

> While my friends are dying cursing God,
> These people go to movies—
>   Nurses
>   In Bataan
> And cry.
> I saw that movie
> And I laughed—
> I could not help myself.[78]

Probably the most important poem, personally and in terms of future work, is also one of the longest and most vivid: "Morituri Te Salutamus."

In this he has a vision of all the dead and wounded from F Company at the assault on the Galloping Horse. The poet finds himself "standing on the Horse," "Brought back in fear & loathing and against my will," forced to stand there while the known dead pass in review before him:

> In solitary line
> As I last saw them:
> Dried mud ground into their green fatigues,
>   gritty to the touch;
> Helmets (those who have them) rusty, caked
>   with mud;
> Sweat streaming down faces twisted with
>   the agony of fear & tension
> They pass by me with stumbling tread,
> And each looks at me reproachfully & sadly;
> They died; I lived—My God!
> Don't they know they are the lucky ones?[79]

There are also a couple of love poems—"To the Woman Who Is Not" and "Ode to a Young Jewess"—together with some hasty notes concerning the creation of the latter poem and events which were to reappear, remembered and transformed, thirty years later in *Whistle*: "Pass with Rabinowitz: Creel Room, Tap Room Claridge: ink sketch of Brig, peom [*sic*] for Jewess. Room 1517 with Rabinowitz & Marie. Over leave next morning. Pass with Rabinowitz was best time I've had."[80]

In *A Friendship* Willie Morris reports that Jones recalled fistfights with sailors (also used in *Whistle*) and a succession of love affairs, including one fairly serious relationship with a young woman who worked at a nearby defense plant. There are, among Jones's papers and letters of this period, a number of references to a particular young woman who worked in the hospital—Adelaide Lawler; but there is no indication that their relationship was any more or less than a friendship.

The service history of James Jones, from the time he arrived back in the United States until his discharge in 1944, is somewhat confusing and further complicated by the fact that it is distributed in fictionalized form among the several characters of *Whistle*. There are a couple of fairly reliable autobiographical sources that cover at least parts of the period in some detail. There is a copy of a letter by Jones in the Scribner's Archives at Princeton, a letter sent from Venice, Florida, January 24, 1948, to Edward Weeks of the *Atlantic*. Weeks had a few days earlier accepted "Temper of Steel" for *Atlantic*. Jones was apparently replying fully to a request for some biographical information. To Weeks he explains that he had spent about nine months in the Memphis hospital, then a brief time back on active duty, before receiving an honorable discharge ("Neuropsychiatric Section II") with a 40 percent disability. There is another letter by Jones, written for reasons that are not at all clear, a very long letter (March 6, 1951, from King's Cottage, Fort Myers Beach, Florida) to Marshall Wingfield, D.D., 246 S. Watkins Street, Memphis, Tennessee.[81] This is the most complete coverage and explanation of Jones's last year in the service that I have seen. He explains that his difficulties with the Army seem to have begun shortly after his arrival at Kennedy General Hospital in May of 1943. He had hoped to receive a thirty-day furlough and to visit his brother in Miami. When this did not develop, he took a furlough anyway (AWOL) and caught a train home to Robinson. This, according to the letter, was the first of three times that he was to go AWOL, the last of which was to cost him his stripes as a corporal and land him in the psychiatric ward of the station hospital at Camp Campbell, Kentucky. When he was originally released from Kennedy Hospital, he says he was given a choice, since his ankle was still a serious disability in spite of the operation and convalescence, of taking a discharge then or continuing in the service on limited duty. He tells the Reverend Dr. Wingfield that he chose to continue to serve as a limited duty soldier. In this accounting, he was assigned to K Company, 101st Infantry, 26th Infantry Division (the old Yankee Division), which was in training, preparing to ship out for England. After a time, and a number of incidents which are reiterated in *Whistle*, he went AWOL again, late in 1943 or very early in 1944. He returned to Robinson. He tells Wingfield that there he had already met and been encouraged by Lowney Handy and that "I was fairly bursting to write." This time when he came back to the Army, he was abruptly restored to full duty, disability or no, and reassigned to the 842nd QM Gas Supply Company. This ragtag company was, except for its officers, composed entirely of veterans of combat in the Pacific and Europe, supposedly disabled and, according to Jones, "a company of cripples." But (as in *Whistle*) their regular duty was hard physical labor. And then someone decided that they should undergo a full six weeks' cycle of basic training.

Lowney Handy, Jones, and Harry Handy, Florida, late 1940s

Jones went "over the hill" for the third time. He felt that the last of his luck was used up. And he knew that when he returned to duty this third time (he had no intention of *deserting* the Army in wartime), he would be busted to private, which is what happened. There was also a good chance —as Landers was to be threatened in *Whistle*—that he might be slapped in the stockade and then immediately transferred overseas as what was called, in *Whistle*, a "recalcitrant replacement."

His uncle, Charles Jones, had been no help. After Jones's first visit to Robinson—during which, to his uncle's acute embarrassment (as Jones saw it, in recounting a similar incident in *Some Came Running*), Jones got drunk and passed out in the sedate Mission Tea Room and ended up spending the night in jail—Jones had tried to get himself transferred somewhere close to Robinson. But he believed that Uncle Charles had pulled strings to *prevent* this. None of this, however, appears in the letter to Wingfield.

Instead, he points out that it was Lowney Handy who took an interest in him. Lowney, thirty-nine at the time they met, in November of 1943, was a native of Marshall, Illinois, the daughter of James Turner, the sheriff of Clark County. Attractive and dynamic, she was married to Harry Handy, who managed the Ohio Oil Refinery in Robinson. Together the couple set to work seriously in Jones's behalf, pulling strings, knocking on doors, using every bit of the not inconsiderable influence they were able to muster. In the Wingfield letter James quotes Lowney as saying to someone in authority, "Only time will tell which is most important, that America not lose the war or that James Jones not be killed in it." He adds that the Handys believe he has the potential to become a great writer, "and that is what I have my sights on becoming, someday, a great writer."

The deal that was worked out for Jones involved a brief stay in the neuropsychiatric ward at the station hospital (where, Jones says, he gathered material for the stockade section of *From Here to Eternity*), followed on July 6, 1944, by a "white discharge"—that is, "Medical & Honorable."

He had not ceased working at his writing, at least not for long. A letter of June 3, 1944, from the return address 842nd QM Gas Supply Company, refers to the novel he is writing, "They Shall Inherit the Laughter."[82]

Lowney Handy was actively encouraging him. She said that "Laughter" had all the ingredients of a best-seller. He aimed for the future with hope and energy. Though he could not have imagined it then, the experiences out of which he would compose his finest and most highly regarded work, the World War II trilogy, had already happened to him. Much lay ahead, a full, interesting, and eventful adult life and an important literary career, but the wounds and blessings, the perceptions and dreams of his spent youth were already in place, destined to serve as the deepest source for all his art.

It has been coming very fast and very well the last three weeks, since I came here, and I've covered a lot of ground that was bothering me. It's a little like walking a tightrope blindfolded with a squirming chicken in each hand.

James Jones[1]

It is amazing, how much good spirits a simple thing like having money can put you in. As soon as I have done the rest of the manuscript, I am taking off from here like a big-assed bird.

James Jones[2]

PART THREE
• • •
BEGINNING

ETERNITY

I don't need to tell you: writing is my life,
if I couldn't write I don't know where the
hell I'd be. But writing without publishing
is like eating without swallowing.

James Jones[3]

.   .   .

JONES was now a civilian, one more among many of the walking
wounded home from the continuing war, but with less to come home to
than most. Restless, angry, confused, and—as he had been when he left
home for the Army but more so now—*hungry* for something. In an undated letter of 1941 (probably May) to Jeff, Jones had written of his
childhood, how he had always been an outsider, had kept to himself in the
school years, adding: "Anyway, it seems I've always felt a hunger and
unrest that nothing could satisfy."[4] Now he wanted more than anything
else to write, and he had the novel he was working on, "They Shall Inherit
the Laughter." This work has now vanished, though much of it was sub-
sumed in other, later work. But Burroughs Mitchell read it in manuscript
at Scribner's and describes it briefly in his *Education of an Editor*. "This
was Jim's first novel, revised after correspondence with Perkins. A clumsy,
ill-proportioned book, describing a soldier AWOL in his hometown during
wartime and raising persistent hell, the novel nevertheless had a power
that impressed us—Perkins, Wheelock, and me."[5]

But even that, the creation of a "clumsy, ill-proportioned book," was still a distant, perhaps unlikely achievement when Jones first came out of the service. He had to educate himself, he had to learn to write. He had to learn so many things he had missed—he even had to learn to drive, a process which would make for a powerful section in *Some Came Running*. Indeed he had no choice but to embrace the old American habit of self-improvement. Learning the things he had missed out on by missing his youth, he learned how to learn things. The rest of his life he was fascinated by trying to learn new skills—skin diving, skiing, the appreciation of art and music, the craft of teaching. And he was curiously confident that he could learn things he set his mind and will to, as, indeed, he did in everything he tried—except the French language, which escaped his best efforts.

He had no job, next to no money, some real responsibilities (he was particularly concerned about the welfare of his younger sister, Tink), and he was under pressure from his Uncle Charles, applying both carrot and stick, to "settle down," to find gainful employment, and to assume his family responsibilities. What he had working for him was a belief in himself and his talent which, coupled with energy and irrepressible desire to succeed, enabled him to overcome the inevitable doubts of himself and his ability that often racked him in spasms of something close to despair.

He also possessed, though he would not know it until it was sorely tested, extraordinary self-discipline, a discipline strong enough to allow him, almost from the outset, to make himself work anywhere and at almost any time, early or late. Years later, close friends like Willie Morris and William Styron would be clearly impressed by his capacity to get up and go to work every morning no matter what had gone on the night before. It was also a self-discipline that permitted him, by an effort of will, to live with his frustration and to overcome his natural impatience. Without that impatience he could not have summoned up the energy to continue working, day in and day out, in the face of indifference and discouragement, a diet of thinnest hopes, frailest expectations. Impatience was strength, then, but it also made each day's work a session on a bed of nails.

But he had other tools for survival also. In the Army, inevitably, he had had to learn to refine the craft and guile of the child in order to endure as painlessly as possible. And this sense of a necessary and deliberate duplicity was intensified by his consciousness—a *self-consciousness*, exaggerated but nonetheless real as the pain of a toothache—that, as he had been a small child, so he was a small man in a world of larger, stronger men. He compensated for this uneasy feeling by cultivating a physical ruggedness and a cocky, athletic swagger—so successfully, in fact, that many people who knew him fairly well remember him as larger, more solid than he ever was. And any number of people who met him briefly remember him as "a big guy." It was more a matter of spirit than of flesh.

Countering all such strategies, however, as if in a kind of inner dialectic, was the brute force and pure power of Jones's overwhelming honesty. Measured against the standards he set for himself, his little masks and disguises might have come to seem so shabby to him (especially in those lean years before he had "accomplished anything") that he would have crippled himself and stifled his potential as a creative artist with a weight of bitter self-contempt. That this common process did not take place, did not happen to him, is the result of a mysterious psychic alchemy. When his integrity touched upon his urgent, *self-conscious* duplicity, the latter was transformed into something else, into *charm*. People remember James Jones as being (at his lowest points as well as his highest) one of the most *charming* men they ever met. The transformation, of course, was gradual. Anger was also close to the surface. As Burroughs Mitchell remembers it: "In these young days, Jim was by no means an easy man. For all the gregariousness, he was strung tight; he could become harsh, even savage, lashing out when something outraged or disgusted him."[6] But even in those "young days," there seems to have been just a wistful touch of irony and self-skepticism behind his bravado which, gave him, as most acquaintances agreed, a very pleasant manner. He was surprisingly gentle (most of the time), and he wore his own troubles like a boutonniere. His interest in other people—something that was noted and remarked on by everyone who knew him and that seems to have been equally applied to all others except for the most outrageously phony or the egregiously foolish—an apparently *genuine* interest, laced with concern and a sense of compassion, came, one imagines, from the need to turn away, to move *outward* from the seething inner life to which his complex nature and mixed gifts condemned him. With a slightly different composition of elements he might have made a successful politician. That may be what Norman Mailer intuitively sensed when he suggested to Mike Wallace, on a television talk show in 1959, that James Jones would make a good President.

Sow's ear to silk purse—his child's guile became pure charm. His inner discontents ironically freed him to look outside, beyond himself, with tact and empathy for others. (It is no wonder that he constructed all of his fiction, beginning with *From Here to Eternity*, from *character* outward, from character to event. Plot came from character and was designed out of the discovery of layers of being, the "truth" of the characters, rather than from the impact of events which, one might imagine, as his characters often do, is supposed to shape character.) The secret key, the magic wand that could turn common pumpkin into shining coach, was honesty. One has the strong feeling that James Jones must have imagined that if he ever told a lie in his art or settled for some cheap and easy truth, then the whole remarkable structure of himself would fall apart. It was this constant threat to his being, in which all his life became a kind of combat situation, that added an extraordinary *intensity* to his charm. It was a gambler's intensity. Intensity on a short leash.

He was conscious of the constant need for self-control. In an essay review of Morris' *James Jones: A Friendship*, Seymour Krim quotes Jones as saying to him, "It's hate and malice that drive the artist on. There are no nice writers."[7] It was as if he wanted to deny the image others derived of him. This was something he said, in a different way, in his acceptance of the National Book Award in 1952. The idea appears to derive from something Maxwell Perkins had written to him.

Sometimes his intensity manifested itself in his appetites. His capacity for drink, while his good health lasted, was legendary and more than likely exaggerated. Jones's Hollywood agent in the 1940s, Ned Brown, reports that the distinguished agent Henry Volkening claimed he and Jones finished off twenty-three stingers at one sitting in a New York restaurant called Cherio's.[8] He could at times eat with equal abandon (and apparently perfect metabolic balance). Shelby Foote recalls a visit by Jones in Greenville, Mississippi, in the early 1950s:

That night we partied and drank till 5 a.m. He was still in his Indian jewelry period and having a lot of trouble with his teeth, but none of it interfered with his appetite. I bet he's still remembered at Jim's Cafe for eating an outsized steak smothered with half a dozen fried eggs, two stacks of lightbread, some five or six cups of coffee, and two helpings of apple pie for dessert. Awe-inspiring—and I forgot the french fries, a whole platter of them eaten along with the steak-and-eggs. Awe-inspiring, I say again. . . .[9]

Jones himself was concerned and conscious of something deeper that this appetite for all the good things of life seemed to symbolize. As he wrote to John Hall Wheelock in a 1950 letter of apology for missing a lunch date: "My whole life seems to be no more than a series of battles against a series of excesses; all kinds of excesses; any excesses; you name it and if I don't have it, I will speedily acquire it."[10]

James Jones was desperately and precariously sane. And that made all the difference.

One thing more made a big difference in those early years—the support and encouragement of the Handys. Harry Handy was well-to-do, the successful executive. Jones described him to Burroughs Mitchell as "the perfect Midwest aristocrat type, somewhat inbred and an absolute gentleman."[11] Handy supported him with $100 a month for some years before Jones began to earn any money from writing; he allowed him to live and work in his own house whenever Jones chose to live in Robinson (and later Marshall); he bought him a jeep and a fine Airstream trailer so that the restless Jones could move about and see the country. And Jones did so, going to and from Florida, the South, and the Southwest, sometimes alone and sometimes in the company of Mrs. Handy. (Willie Morris calls Harry Handy "an understanding soul."[12]) In short, the Handys helped to commission and support the creation of Jones's first novel. Of course, Jones repaid them in full and more after the great commercial success of *From Here to Eternity*. And he was faithful also in gratitude and loyal friendship until, by mid-1957, friendship became no longer possible. But neither he nor they could do more at first than gamble on his uncertain future. That wager was a remarkable gesture. Harry did it, evidently, because he liked James Jones a great deal and, with no children of his own, easily assumed a kind of paternal role with the young man. But Harry also did it to please his wife, Lowney. She had often helped and encouraged young men, and Jones was a particular challenge for her.

Younger than Harry and some seventeen years older than Jones, Lowney came from a large family. She seems to have been interested in many things, fairly well read, and full of ideas and theories. In a revealing *Life* article about her written after the initial success of *From Here to Eternity*, A. B. C. Whipple described her at the time she met Jones, as "a childless housewife of Robinson, Ill., who was looking for someone to mother and who was perceptive enough to see what had escaped editors, teachers and even Jones himself." Whipple said she had been, as a girl, "an

Lowney Handy and Montgomery Clift

OPPOSITE TOP: *Jones's study in the Handy house, late 1940s*

OPPOSITE BOTTOM: *Jones during his "cowboy boots —turquoise/silver phase," mid-1950s*

uninhibited tomboy," and he described her in 1951, when there were a number of young men, called the Group, forming the Handy Artists Group, as being as good an athlete as any of them: "With the football on the beach she can throw a pass as far and run as fast as anyone in the Group." He depicted her, not without enthusiasm, as a demanding mentor, a tough-talking manager of the lives of her Group, possessed of a quick and violent temper.[13]

Among Jones's papers, there are a few letters from her which seem to imply something more in the relationship than Mother-muse-mentor-drill-sergeant-and-tomboy-buddy. And Willie Morris, who talked to Jones (and to Gloria Jones) about this, simply states that when they met "they began an affair that lasted well into the 1950's, more or less with the knowledge of the husband."[14] Certainly the community seems to have assumed it was an affair. In a notebook preserved at the Beinecke, Jones noted that his Uncle Charles, ever (in Jones's view) the prisoner of respectability, disapproved of "the situation." "When I asked him what he meant by 'situation' at Handys, he told me a young man in the same house with the wife of a man who was gone all day."

After the Whipple article had appeared, a Hollywood entrepreneur telegraphed Lowney, who shared the telegram and her amusement with Jones:

VERY EXCITED ABOUT THE LIFE ARTICLE ON YOU AND JONES. FEEL THAT THIS STORY HAS GREAT MOTION PICTURE VALUE AND SHOULD BE TOLD ON THE SCREEN, CERTAIN THAT I CAN INTEREST MAJOR COMPANY IN MAKING PICTURE BASED ON THIS MATERIAL. WOULD APPRECIATE WIRE FROM YOU AUTHORIZING US TO PROCEED.[15]

Whatever the real nature of their intimate relationship (if it can be determined, if it matters), there was, at least for a long time, a certain core of innocence about it, at least from Jones's point of view. In response to a criticism by Josephine Herbst, contained in a letter of overwhelming praise for *Eternity*, that he doesn't know much about women yet, Jones writes to Burroughs Mitchell: "Logically, there *must* be some Amer. women who have sexuality and warmth without being whores. It stands to reason. . . . The only thing is you can't write about something you haven't seen." Later in the same letter he adds: "Lowney says I, like most—nay, all—Amer.

males, am looking for a disembodied angel composed of equal parts of mother and whore—but private whore, you understand."[16]

The situation was complex enough that Jones dealt with it twice in novels, for Lowney stood as the model for Gwen French in *Some Came Running* and Carol Abernathy in *Go to the Widow-Maker*. In both cases critics have claimed difficulty in *believing* these characters; and some characteristics and events which have been seriously questioned by the critics, or held up as ridiculously crude invention, seem to be very close to plain truth. It may be that you had to see Lowney Handy to believe her. Poet David Ray, who was once a member of the Handy Artists Colony and has written a number of pieces about it, has intense and vivid recollections of her and writes that she "scared me to the guts, and Jones too, I think, since he fled the country & had his things sold after he faced her anger when he told her he was going to leave in order to marry."

He continues:

> I cannot possibly convey to you the intensity of Lowney's power. It was charismatic and demonic. Since she used some of the same brain-washing methods to assure the loyalty of her young disciples and was from the same part of the country, I've often wondered if the James Jones of Jonesville knew of her, or perhaps visited her. . . . She was a very violent woman, and unyielding in her jealous possessiveness of her charges, of whom Jones was the chief one. Her control of the community was legend: I saw her tell the Chief of Police what to do, and she boasted of being "above good and evil." She may well have been. Anyway, to understand Jones you have to understand Lowney and the intensity of their relationship.[17]

It is uncertain, a matter for speculation among those who knew them then (or knew of them later), how much a part Lowney Handy played in Jones's development as a writer. As early as the summer of 1950, he seems to have felt—accurately, one imagines—that he would have written anyway, but that "I know I never would have written neither what nor as much as I have had she not stood over me with the club, like the mother standing over the future concertmaster as he sits at the piano [*sic*] with one eye on the clock."[18]

During 1945, from January to June, Jones was living and working in

New York. He took a writing course at NYU under Public Law 15—the Veterans Vocational Rehabilitation Program. It had to be labeled a journalism course, because the law did not recognize creative writing as leading toward a gainful occupation (the G.I. Bill had not yet come into being). But his adviser, Frank H. McCloskey, helped him bend the law so that he could work on his fiction. Jones had come to New York to finish up a full draft of "They Shall Inherit the Laughter," and to try to find an agent and a publisher for it. He found an agent without much difficulty. A letter of introduction took him to Maxwell and Ruth Aley, who had a son just about his age serving in Europe and took an instant liking to him. And they were impressed by his work and potential. In point of fact, plenty of people were recognizing that Jones had talent. Some thought he had the potential to be a fine writer. But nobody seemed able to help him much, not even the Aleys, who represented him, more or less officially, throughout 1945 and 1946. Even though the Aleys could not, in the end, do anything much for Jones, their interest and encouragement must have been a help at a difficult time.[19]

Jones had good luck in finding an interested publisher. A. Scott Berg's biography of Maxwell Perkins describes Jones as one of Perkins' last "discoveries." Berg's account, based in part on interviews and correspondence with Jones, has Jones arrive carrying the manuscript of "They Shall Inherit the Laughter" in "a string-tied Eaton Bond box" to the fifth floor editorial offices of Scribner's. Through the kindness of an elderly receptionist, he was allowed to deliver it to Perkins personally and have a long and serious talk with him. Perkins took a liking to him and an interest in his work. Scribner's did not make an offer for "Laughter" as it stood at that point. But neither did Perkins discourage Jones from rewriting and revising the novel in an effort to get it into shape for publication. After finishing up the semester at NYU, Jones spent the summer living in the mountains of North Carolina, then returned to Robinson and subsequently to Florida, where he worked part-time, at night, on a charter fishing boat and continued the revisions of his novel. On January 17, 1946, while staying with Jeff and his family in Tallahassee, Jones resubmitted the manuscript of "Laughter" to Perkins. Although, except for a receipt, he heard nothing at all for a while from Perkins, he was confident enough already to claim success in a letter to his old teacher in Hawaii—Dr. Carl Stroven. "My first novel, which I referred to in my letter to Dr. Schwartz, is—as far as I know now—coming out in April," Jones wrote. "Maxwell Perkins, whom I met in New York, is publishing it for Scribner's. At least that's the way it looks right now. The book is titled: 'They Shall Inherit the Laughter'."[20] Six days later, still having heard nothing from Perkins or Scribner's, Jones wrote a long letter, politely asking what was happening and advising Perkins that he was "champing at the bit" to get started on his next novel. He presented a number of ideas and wondered which of these might interest Perkins most as a good subject for a book to follow "Laughter." The first of these (which Jones said came to him after "seeing the movie of A Walk in the Sun and reading several reviews of the book") was to be "a real combat novel, telling the complete truth, or as near the complete truth as a writer can ever approach." And he was interested in the notion of a novel about "a man who has fulfilled all the obligations asked him by society," but who fails to prosper in society. Another idea, evidently based on some events at Harry Handy's refinery, was a novel dealing with "strikes." His second idea for the next novel, immediately following his enthusiastic discussion of the "real combat novel" was to be a novel chiefly about a soldier named Stewart, somewhat in the manner of an up-to-date *What Price Glory* and dealing with the Army in peacetime. "I have always wanted to do a novel on the peacetime army," James wrote, "something I don't remember having seen."[21]

In New York Perkins had decided to reject "Laughter." Unhappy with it but uncertain of his own reaction, he had asked Scribner's newest young editor, a war veteran named Burroughs Mitchell, to read the manuscript and report on it. Mitchell was impressed by Jones's "considerable force" and "considerable story-telling gift." "I don't think the novel should be accepted in its present shape," the memo concluded. "But I was really impressed by it. It is a far more honest and accurate book than a number of far more professional things that have been published about war problems."[22] Perkins decided to decline the manuscript but to encourage Jones as a writer, using a method which was then popular at Scribner's and other publishing houses. This involved a relatively simple "first refusal" agreement; that is, instead of offering a contract for publication, the publishing house paid the author a few hundred dollars for an option on an idea, with the possibility, if the property should develop well, of offering a contract on the completed work. Thus, for a good deal less than a normal advance, the publisher took a chance on the author's coming through with something publishable and in return acquired temporary ownership of the putative work. The author, presumably, would be pleased—some interest was better than no interest at all, and money of any sort is always proof of genuine support.

On the morning of February 16, 1946, Maxwell Perkins sent Jones the following telegram:

> WOULD YOU CONSIDER PAYMENT FIVE HUNDRED NOW FOR OPTION ON STEWART NOVEL AND SETTING ASIDE INHERIT LAUGHTER FOR REASONS ILL WRITE SOME FURTHER PAYMENT TO BE MADE AFTER WE APPROVE SOME FIFTY THOUSAND WORDS. WISH TO COOPERATE BUT HAVE MORE FAITH IN SECOND NOVEL AND HAVE FURTHER REVISION TO PROPOSED [sic] FOR LAUGHTER[23]

Jones had returned to Robinson on February 15. He received the telegram, thought about it, and wired back on the 17: PROPOSITION ACCEPTED PLACING MYSELF IN YOUR HANDS AND AWAITING LETTER HERE. . . .[24]

It was natural, almost inevitable, that Jones would be drawn toward Maxwell Perkins—editor for Wolfe, Fitzgerald, and Hemingway among others—and an old-fashioned publisher like Scribner's. It was natural for him to believe in them, to trust their judgment. It is true that somebody else might conceivably have offered him a contract for "They Shall Inherit the Laughter." One other publisher did see it and rejected it; but other people in the business read it and were impressed. For instance, among Jones's papers at the Beinecke Library, there is a memo of October 5, 1945, from the Story Department of 20th Century-Fox, praising "Laughter" for its "power, sincerity, real feeling for character" and adding that "Jones conveys emotion with considerable force." But the option contract was terribly important to Jones at that stage, an enormous encouragement, and so much so that he never imagined that Scribner's was routinely paying him a small fee to see if there might possibly be anything to his idea for a novel about the peacetime Army. Perhaps if Jones had understood that lots of writers in those days were being hooked by publishers for small options which committed the writer without seriously committing the publisher to anything much, he might have been more easily discouraged in the long chore of putting *Eternity* together. But the option and the interest Perkins showed were all he needed, at that time, to continue to give his life to his writing and to dedicate himself to this one subject. He took the option as a testament of faith in him and his talent—which happened to be exactly what he needed in order to endure and prevail.

And so the creation of *From Here to Eternity* began. With it began as well one of the most interesting examples of literary correspondence between author and editors that I know of, first between Jones and Perkins, then after Perkins' death (June 18, 1947), between Jones and his new editor—Burroughs Mitchell. By 1950, when John Hall Wheelock put together a representative selection of the letters of Maxwell Perkins for book publication, Jones's gifts were well enough known at Scribner's that, even though *Eternity* was still being written, a couple of Perkins' letters to the young writer were included in the book.[25] Jones later told Harvey Breit that he had actually met with Perkins only twice.[26] For the relatively short time they knew each other and Perkins served as Jones's editor, their correspondence was extensive. And Perkins saw some two hundred pages of an early draft of the novel, including a preliminary version of the celebrated scene where Prewitt ("Stewart") plays taps at Schofield Barracks, which Perkins much admired.

After hearing from Perkins—who spoke of "Laughter" more as a matter of *timing* than anything else, and left open the possibility of returning to it later—Jones set to work on the new book. It was a strange and difficult experience for him. "I'm stumbling along in the dark," he wrote Perkins, "and there seems to be nobody to teach me what I must learn in the manner in which history is taught to a history student."[27] A year later he was clearer about what his chief problem was:

> I'm having troubles I never had before. LAUGHTER was largely auto-biographical and I had a readymade plot and characters who followed it; all I had to do was heighten it and use my imagination. But here I have nothing to go on except certain people I knew in the army and what made them tick. There is no plot at all except what I can create.[28]

The original scheme of the novel called for three sections: the first, "1930–Dec 7/41"; second, "Dec 7–Nov 42"; third "Nov 42–Death of Prewitt" on New Georgia.[29] Prewitt would survive combat on Guadalcanal and New Georgia only to get drunk and drown in a river. But by the time he wrote Perkins a sixteen-page letter on March 16, 1947, Jones had decided to limit the time scheme of the story from April through December of 1941. In this letter he decides to abandon the "major wartime Hawaii part for a later book."

He had had the title by October 21, 1946, one that everybody was happy with, though it took Perkins to tell him it came originally from Kipling and not from the Yale "Whiffenpoof Song." On July 30, 1946, the original option was renewed. Scribner's had now invested $1,000 in the project. Slowly the novel was taking shape, as can be traced in the letters back and forth between Jones and Perkins. On June 23, 1947, Jones wrote a five-page letter to Perkins in which, among other things, he advanced the idea of perhaps following this first novel with a collection of short stories. Perkins was dead before Jones wrote and mailed the letter. No one had thought to tell him. He heard the news from Burroughs Mitchell.[30] In *The Education of an Editor* Mitchell quotes at length from Jones's reply to him of June 30, 1947, in which Jones explains how Scribner's and Perkins had already become a kind of family for him.

> My parents both died when I was overseas, which is probably just as well, and the relatives I do have are estranged from me over the question of whether I should go to work or write. That includes my uncle and my sister and lately my brother, who are the only ones left now. And so I have sort of had for Scribner's and for him and his faith in me the feeling a young man usually has for home.[31]

Jones asked to work with Mitchell, which was fine with Scribner's.

And so began a friendship that lasted until Jones's death—and along with it a very extensive and detailed correspondence, about life and art and everything, but chiefly about the given manuscript in progress, a correspondence which was to continue as an *official* matter until Jones left Scribner's in 1964. Most of these letters are filed and preserved in the Charles Scribner's Archives at Princeton. They detail the growth and development, from inception to finished books, and the reactions of the reviewers, of *From Here to Eternity, Some Came Running, The Pistol, The Thin Red Line.* Jones was some 150 pages into the writing of *Go to the Widow-Maker* when he left Scribner's.

But when Perkins died, Jones had a long way to go. He would not complete the writing of *Eternity*, or receive a contract for it, for nearly three years. He was still six months away from the publication of *anything* that he had written.

Every writer works alone but within a complex literary situation. Complex because the literary situation is—and certainly was *then*, in those postwar years—constantly changing, rearranging itself; complex also because in large part the writer at his lonely craft cannot really know the hard facts, let alone "the truth" about the publishing world to which he must sooner or later take his "product." It is as if some old-fashioned subsistence farmer with horse and wagon and wagonload of produce were setting out to do some business with one of the major chains of supermarkets. So the writer does what writers always do as part of their very craft. He imagines a literary situation and then elects to live in it. Success or failure often depends a good deal on the extent to which this imaginary literary situation turns out to correspond with anything in reality. It is clear now that, at the beginning, Jones really thought he was living and working in approximately the world inhabited by Hemingway, Faulkner, Fitzgerald, Wolfe, Steinbeck, and Dos Passos. This sense of unbroken continuity was seemingly confirmed by the gradual republication of their work at that time. The Viking Portable Library editions of some of these masters were just coming along. Jones bought them and kept them handy. People who remember Jones from the forties and fifties recall those Viking Portables, which he cheerfully called his "influences."

Jones was part of another literary situation, an attempt by American publishers to launch the next wave of writers, to establish a postwar generation of novelists. That was one of the new things about America, the wonderfully confident assumption that in all activities, even the arts, we could now shape history rather than passively wait for it to happen. Very soon, in the decade of the 1950s, the Beat Generation would prove, with considerable success, that an entire literary movement could be fabricated, could be announced and then created, as much by publicity as creativity, and that it could be taken as seriously (even by those who had created it) as if it had happened spontaneously. It was apparent to many of the new men of the new America, publishers and writers among them, that it is far more sensible (and profitable) to arrange for movements and "discoveries" in advance than to wait upon variable, unpredictable circumstances. Jones's "Laughter" had been rejected, Perkins told him in several letters, primarily because of timing and the feeling that the subject matter was not commercial. *Eternity* offered something special and different.

What Jones could not have imagined, even if he had been fairly sophisticated in such things, was what other people were up to at the same time. Looking back now, we can see that many other writers were then busily creating their war novels. The 1950s would be freighted with them. And the late forties, the very years Jones was writing *Eternity*, had seen some first-rate work, including Heggen's *Mister Roberts* (1946), Michener's Pulitzer Prize–winning *Tales of the South Pacific* (1947), Mailer's *The Naked and the Dead* (1948), Shaw's *The Young Lions* (1948), and James Gould Cozzens' Pulitzer Prize–winning *Guard of Honor* (1948). Scribner's had brought out its own war novel in 1947—Vance Bourjaily's *The End of My Life*. The idea of yet another war novel, by an unknown, could not have been greatly appealing. But . . . the idea of a novel dealing with the peacetime Army, with an America still remembered but lost now beyond recovering, the idea of *From Here to Eternity* as it was slowly taking shape, *that* was new and different. It just might work if the young man managed somehow to put together a coherent story.

Jones's letters and notes show that he worked on the book steadily for the next four years. Sometimes, after he had submitted a batch of manuscript pages to Mitchell and was left waiting awhile, he would work on short stories, hoping to get something published to show for himself. In April 1949, with a number of stories already published or accepted, he suggested to Mitchell the idea of Scribner's doing a book of stories in advance of *Eternity*.[32] A little later that same month he tested the waters again, casually wondering whether his *next book*, after *Eternity*, should be a collection of stories or a novel.[33] Scribner's was having none of that at the time or, for that matter, later; for Sribner's never proposed publication of a collection of Jones's stories. (That same letter to Mitchell outlines a planned novel which sounds very much like *Whistle*.)

He wrote his stories during brief rest and rehabilitation periods and started sending them around himself. (Later Mitchell would help him place them.) Jones had worked out a kind of standard letter to accompany the stories. He introduced himself, usually as a protégé of the late Maxwell Perkins and as a writer under contract at Scribner's. He then offered the editor (or agent) in question a golden opportunity to take (or to represent) one or more outstanding short stories. He usually added that, unlike Hemingway and Faulkner, he had no plan to *resubmit* these stories to them after he was established. He was allowing them one chance and one chance only, and this was it. Surprisingly, a good many distinguished and experienced editors took him seriously. Maybe they were simply bored and jaded and were amused at the innocent novelty of his approach. But it also appears that they sensed the power, the energy, and the talent in both the letters and the stories. There is a letter from *Harper's* to Burroughs Mitchell which simply states: "All of us here feel that he has as much promise as any writer whose work we have seen in the last year."[34] Jones tells about the fates of some of these early stories in *The Ice-Cream Head-ache.* What he does not tell there (or anywhere else) is how both then and later, when he had "arrived," he literally terrorized editors about making any changes at all in his copy.

Here, for example, is an unsigned memo, of April 11, 1951, addressed to Charlotte McBride and preserved among the *"Esquire* Magazine Office Files," of the Arnold Gingrich papers at the University of Michigan:

> As you've probably heard Jones (who is the hottest guy in the writing business right now) will not permit his copy to be changed, and won't permit the use of the apostrophe in words like wont [*sic*]. Therefore we've had it typed exactly as he wrote it.[35]

There are many other examples of Jones's authorial stubbornness, in large matters and small, throughout his correspondence.

As for the novel, he kept at it and kept moving as he wrote. Back and forth from Illinois to Florida (Venice, Fort Myers, Marathon). He would hitch up his trailer, hit the road, stop some place, and settle down to work for a while. Letters and manuscript pages come and go from Memphis, Henderson (Arkansas), Tucson, Albuquerque, Colorado Springs, North Hollywood. One of the things, together with his Viking Portable Library books, which Jones carried with him was a folded, well-thumbed clipping from the *New York Times Book Review* of January 4, 1948: "Best Sellers: How They Are Made," by Harvey Breit.

As he got closer to the end of it, through the summer and fall of 1949, his letters began to be dotted with complaints about his health, a case of flu, the circulatory numbness of his hands. An ear infection in Henderson (August 3, 1949) put him in the hospital for four days. He wrote Mitchell from Tucson that he was having "hemerrhoid troubles." But troubles or not, he managed in the same letter to crank out ideas for five more novels, one of which is clearly going to become *Some Came Running,* the chief theme of which was to be found, Jones said, in the dilemma of the protagonist who "would rather have a steady piece of ass than be a writer."[36]

By August 16, 1949, he had written 1,076 manuscript pages of *Eternity*, which he had long since named "the great endless American novel." On October 30, 1949, he sent in the Pearl Harbor section. It was almost done. He was finished with a revised draft of the novel by the end of February 1950. Actually, he had submitted the final sections earlier; for he had heard in Tucson from John Hall Wheelock (December 5, 1949) that he had just finished reading the manuscript and "I can't resist telling you how deeply moved, and excited, I have been by this splendid, often beautiful, often terrible book. It is an achievement of the first order and one I believe will be so recognized."[37] In due time, April 21, 1950, a contract came along, offering an advance of $2,500, of which $2,250 had already been paid in options. It was a perfectly conventional contract except that Scribner's took only 10 percent of any motion picture rights after the agent's commission. Jones kept moving and working on the novel, in galley proof and page proof. Scribner's began to get the idea that this book was not only a very good one, but possibly a commercial "property" as well. And then things began to happen rather quickly.

In September Jones had to come to New York to meet with the lawyer for Scribner's, Horace S. Manges of Weil, Gotshal & Manges. There was the problem of the language of *Eternity* and the law. Author and lawyer sat down with the manuscript and negotiated. Jones sent letters to his friends describing what happened. Here he tells "Woodie" (Pfc. Robert E. Harris) how it went: "The lawyer had a scoresheet. There were 259 fucks, 92 shits, and 5 pricks. He didn't count the pisses for some reason. . . . We finally ended up by whittling the scoresheet down to 106 fucks, probably 35 shits and still 5 pricks."[38] On November 27, 1950, back at home, Jones sent greetings to Manges via Mitchell: "Just tell him Jones asked to be remembered to that fucking lawyer."[39]

After *Eternity* Manges became Jones's lawyer and over the years found plenty of things, above and beyond dirty words, to keep him busy.

In October, Scribner's gave Jones another $2,000, which represented the advance on a "proposed novel" (to be *Some Came Running*). In November he learned that the Book-of-the-Month Club had chosen *Eternity* as an alternate selection. It would have been the main selection, Mitchell told him, except that they feared the language might bring them trouble with the Post Office. Also in November, he got a first look at the design for the book jacket. On the thirteenth he wrote Mitchell that he liked the proposed jacket fine, but he hoped it might be possible to make a couple of changes. He thought that professional soldiers should have better haircuts and should look a little less wrinkled and rumpled. Moreover, he was unhappy about the inaccuracy of the uniform. "We did not wear 'cunt-caps' [the overseas cap] in the Hawaiian Dept. until sometime after the war started. . . ." Nor did troops in Hawaii wear blouses. "We wore summer uniforms exclusively which is CKC [cotton khaki cloth] shirts and pants; and for dress uniforms we wore the same with wool OD [olive drab] garrison caps, the ones with visors. But for undress uniforms we wore the same again, except the garrison caps were exchanged for campaign hats."[40] Scribner's wasn't much concerned about the authenticity of uniforms. The jacket stayed the same. But they did use his own biographical notes. And their jacket text was unequivocal in its claims for literary excellence: "The publishers believe that the appearance of this novel is of comparable importance to the publication of *This Side of Paradise* or *Look Homeward, Angel*."

By December 6, 1950, Mitchell was warning Jones of potential tax problems and advising him to get a good tax consultant.

On December 16 Scribner's took the cover of *Publishers Weekly* with a paid advertisement, featuring a picture of the young James Jones looking tough and muscular in a striped T-shirt. People were already talking deals; and suddenly everything had changed for him. After seeing the cover of *Publishers Weekly*, with full-page ads on the following pages, Jones was swept by a sad awareness that something was all over for him. He wrote Mitchell about it on Christmas Eve, 1950:

> After I got my ego back to normal from the picture (which is much to [sic] handsome) and the ad's buildup, I discovered that in the process I had lost "Eternity." It wasn't mine any more. All the work and fear and sweat and blood, and you know I am not romanticizing, it all went for nothing now. . . . And now it is only just another book, to be laid on shelves and handled by prospective customers and maybe bought, and even read, yet with that all, still it is just another book.[41]

Running close to nine hundred pages in print, *From Here to Eternity* is large in scope and ambition as well as size, a "major" novel by any useful definition of that term. It is structured in five related and chronological sequences—"The Transfer," "The Company," "The Women," "The Stockade," and "The Re-Enlistment Blues," each one of which has almost the length and weight of a conventional novel. In effect, it is the story of the peacetime Army, as Jones had experienced it, set in Hawaii's Schofield Barracks, at the tag end of the Great Depression, a time of our history which ended suddenly and permanently with the Japanese attack on Pearl Harbor. That attack, brilliantly handled by Jones from the limited point of view of his characters, comes near the end of the novel; and everything begins changing quickly before our eyes, a radical sense of change enhanced by the fact that we know what none of these characters can imagine—the long, bloody road to victory in World War II and the end of much that seemed inherently characteristic of American life. The small, isolated Army, caste-ridden with its hierarchy of bourgeois officer class and its proletarian enlisted men, riddled with all its intense and petty peacetime concerns, was soon to be exploded and utterly transformed by the influx of millions of civilian soldiers, who came not to make careers out of soldiering but only to fight and win a war and then to go home. On the one hand, a strong appeal of the novel is to be found in its accurate recapturing of the Army just as it was before the storm, a way of life not known to many Americans, therefore new and strange enough to them to be very interesting, even among those who, by the end of the war, had spent more time in the service than Jones. On the other hand, the texture of the times was so well represented by Jones that the book partook of a much larger, shared nostalgia, the awareness of loss and of the permanent changes which accompanied the traumatic experience of the war. Centered chiefly around a single infantry company, G Company stationed at Schofield Barracks, its officers and its men and the women (in some cases shared) of both classes, the story is told with great energy and power and in a clear, strong, lively language, disdainful of euphemisms. This was a use of language which had seldom been seen in popular American fiction and never before with such overt emphasis. The other postwar novelists, every one of them, Mailer included, had dodged the issue of accurately presenting G.I. English. (Mailer used the euphemism "fug" in *The Naked and the Dead*.) After *Eternity*, for better and for worse, the American novel was never to be as inhibited as it had been before.

But mainly, in a book crowded with well-realized characters of all kinds, villainous and admirable alike, *Eternity* introduced the trinity of central characters who preside, under various names, throughout Jones's trilogy of World War II novels—Robert E. Lee Prewitt, former bugler and boxer; Sgt. Milton Anthony Warden, first sergeant of G Company, and Sgt. Maylon Stark, mess sergeant. Prewitt and Warden emerge as multidimensional and altogether memorable figures, each sharing mythological, archetypal American qualities, each a strong-willed, stubborn loner and a rebel in his own way, and each paying a heavy price for his individualism and rebellion—yet each one a superbly capable, dedicated soldier, each at war with the "system," while loving the Army. These two are complex characters whose roots are as deep in our historical consciousness as in our literature; and the tragedies that beset them—the loss of love by Warden, the loss of his life by Prewitt—are shattering and, in a strictly artistic sense, completely satisfying.

Although it was surely not planned this way, except insofar as Jones intended to create, if possible, the illusion of a *complete* world within the limits of his story, there was something for almost everyone in *Eternity*. If political and social conservatives could read it for the sake of historical nostalgia, the intellectual left read it for its social criticism and for its apparently solid ideological foundations. The literati could rejoice in its vitality, its range of vernacular language, its elegant and deceptively simple structure, its exploration of the American psyche, and, above all, in its successful marriage of the concerns of serious fiction with the pleasures of popular fiction. But more important than the reactions of any of these special interest groups was the reaction of huge numbers of readers who read it (and still do) for the power and the validity of a story they could believe, about people who mattered, written by a new American writer who seemed wonderfully fresh and worthwhile.

T H E publication of *From Here to Eternity* is one of the great success stories of American publishing in our time.

(It should be at least mentioned that it was an enormous *foreign* success also. The book was published by William Collins Sons in Britain, as were Jones's later books. Likewise it was published in German, French, Italian, Danish, Yiddish, Swedish, Spanish, Dutch, Norwegian, Serbo-Croatian, and Polish editions.)

The paperback reprint rights went to New American Library for

Eternity *jacket photos, fall 1950*

From Here to Eternity *poster*

Donna Reed, Montgomery Clift, Frank Sinatra, and Fred Zinnemann in From Here to Eternity

$119,000 (which Jones and Scribner's split fifty-fifty). In spite of the prospect of serious difficulties that caused some film producers to turn it down —a memo to Harry Cohn, who in fact produced *Eternity*, lists "four major sources of potential trouble: military, censorship problems, political, and religion"[42]—Columbia Pictures acquired the motion picture rights to *Eternity* on March 16, 1951. What this meant, among other things, was that Jones would receive payments of $20,000 on each January 2 for the next three years, plus some additional money for helping with the script and for consultation.

By April 27, 1951, two months after publication, the estimate was that 125,000 copies of the hardcover edition of *Eternity* had been sold. And there was no end in sight. When *Some Came Running* was published in 1958, the publisher offered the following information on the book jacket: "The hard-cover edition of *From Here to Eternity*, James Jones [*sic*] first novel, has now sold five hundred thousand copies in this country; the paperbound edition over three million." By 1963 Jones was able to total his earnings from Scribner's, on *From Here to Eternity* alone, as $388,329.61.

It is hard to imagine a critical response to the book that could have been better. The typical review was "mixed," in the sense that there were minor reservations about the language, the brutality of some scenes, and the sex; but these reservations were seen by one reviewer after another as overwhelmingly outweighed by the veracity and vitality of the novel. The standard, in tone and argument, may fairly be taken from the review by Gene Baro in the *New York Herald Tribune* Book Review. " 'From Here to Eternity' is in some ways a difficult book for it faces squarely the agonies of our time. It has a directness, a force, a vigor that cannot be described. Many will think it too brutal. It has no more brutality than a daily newspaper. It is a work appropriate to our age, a novel in the tradition of free inquiry."[43] The *Library Journal* notice called it "powerful and substantial" and, predicting it to be a best-seller, added that in all probability "this is an outstanding novel of enduring worth."[44] David Dempsey praised it highly in the *New York Times Book Review*, stating that "an original and utterly honest talent has restored American realism to a preeminent place in world literature."[45] So did C. J. Rolo in *Atlantic* ("it has tremendous vitality and driving power and graphic authenticity")[46] and Ned Calmer in *Saturday Review*.[47] Robert P. Jordan in *The Washington Post* ("It Makes You Sick But Proud") typically regretted the language, but celebrated the novel:

It is Jones' faithful reporting, of which these words are a part, that gives the novel its extreme and, at times, terrible realism. It, too, is Jones' deep understanding of the Army and the men in it that makes the novel human and appealing. It is his communication of the brotherhood of man and man's inhumanity to man that brings the novel close to greatness.[48]

Jones even found himself and his book as subjects on the Editorial page of *Life* ("From Here to Obscenity"), in which, after some moderate fuming against the language, *Life* concluded it was a good book and set it against Mailer's war novel: "Its vigor, its sincerity, and a fundamental understanding of the respect for the Army set this novel apart from such insidious slime as 1948's *The Naked and the Dead*."[49]

Even the negative reviews, all perhaps except for Bernard DeVoto's attack in *Harper's* ("Dull Novels Make Dull Reading"),[50] were properly respectful. For example, Robie Macauley's "Private Jones's Revenge" in *Kenyon Review*, while asserting that "half of the book seems to have been extracted from grade B movies," ended his piece on a fairly positive note: "Overpraised as it has been, it is neither a bad book nor a typical bestseller." Adding: "All of its virtues of energy and indignation should not be denied."[51] In *The Nation* Ernest Jones called it "preposterously overpraised."[52] Even one of the boldest attacks against Jones's ability and the book, Leslie Fiedler's essay in *Commentary* ("James Jones' Dead-End Young Werther: The Bum as Cultural Hero") acknowledged "the authority of the documentation that is forever saving the book from its own ambitions," adding that "its value as literature . . . lies in redeeming for the imagination aspects of regular army life never before exploited, and in making of certain of those aspects (the stockade, for instance, our homegrown concentration camp) symbols of the human situation everywhere."[53]

By the time the movie of *Eternity* had appeared in 1953 and had achieved a great commercial success, winning for itself six academy awards (Best Picture, Fred Zinneman for direction, Daniel Taradash for screenplay, Barnett Guffey for cinematography, Frank Sinatra for Best Supporting Actor, and Donna Reed for Best Supporting Actress), the story and the characters of *From Here to Eternity* were part of the folklore of the age.

Since that time there have been many critical assaults on specific books by Jones and, indeed, on the nature and limits of Jones's gifts, yet even these critics seem to feel the need to pause to praise *Eternity*. There are very few subsequent attacks on *Eternity* itself. Harvey Swados allowed himself a brief attack in his *New Republic* massacre of *Some Came Running* ("Through a Glass Sourly Darkly"), calling *Eternity* "sentimentally conceived and crudely written."[54] In *College English*, John T. Frederick called *Eternity* "a steaming tubful of sex and sadism for the appetite of the same readers that have made Mickey Spillane and the later Erskine Caldwell all time best-sellers."[55] But in that same issue of that journal Richard P. Adams ("A Second Look at *From Here to Eternity*") called Jones "a major talent" and added: "He penetrates to the very center of the most important cultural, political, and philosophical questions of our day."[56] And more recent studies are based upon the firm assumption of the literary importance of *Eternity*. In *War and the Novelist: Appraising the American War Novel* (1976), Peter G. Jones writes, "In spite of some weaknesses, *From Here to Eternity* is the best modern American war novel, one of the finest novels of the twentieth century."[57]

On January 29, 1952, together with the other two winners—Marianne Moore (*Collected Poems*) and Rachel Carson (*The Sea Around Us*)—James Jones was presented with a National Book Award, its citation praising the "passionate honesty and profound feeling" of his work. He had overcome some formidable competition for the prize, J. D. Salinger's *The Catcher in the Rye* and Herman Wouk's *The Caine Mutiny* among them. Jones raised a few eyebrows, especially among his middle-American constituency, with what Lon Tinkle of the *Dallas Morning News* called "a startling acceptance speech." The *Nashville Tennessean* showed Jones in a photograph, arm in arm with Mickey Spillane, and quoted him as saying: "The only thing wrong with literature in our time is that it lacks the proper proportion of malice, envy, and hate."[58] Tinkle also quoted Jones as saying: "It seems to me that the weary futility and deep depression we all hate to see in our literature today are caused by this fear of rascality in our writers which is unwittingly turning them into moralists."[59]

Nobody imagined he was quoting the late Maxwell Perkins. Some papers wondered out loud if the fiction judges had not made a big mistake.[60]

The truth is, I'm scared to death of it. I've
been making copious notes, and doing much
thinking. But I just haven't quite got up the
nerve yet to jump. If it comes out as I want
it to come out, it will do for 20th Century
American "Love" what Stendhal did for the
18th Century French. That's the aim,
anyway, however far short it falls.

James Jones[61]

Anyway, I'm much more interested in your
opinion of RUNNING than in what all of them
say about it, good or bad. . . . Everything
about that book was deliberate—the heavy,
involved style and syntax, as well as the
loose sprawling quality of the narrative—
and all flaws are flaws of commission; all
done in an effort to reach a further
expression.

James Jones[62]

.   .   .

WHAT happened next, depending on point of view, is powerfully simple
or elaborately complex.

In the simple version, Jones returned home to Illinois and, with some
appropriate and necessary changes such as building a house near Marshall
on a lot adjoining a 400-acre farm owned by the Handys, tried to take up
the life he had followed during the years of writing *Eternity*. He wrote his
second novel, *Some Came Running*, finishing a full draft in 1956. About
that time, thanks to Budd Schulberg, he met Gloria Mosolino and fell in

love with her. Gloria came from Pottsville, Pennsylvania, had attended Syracuse University, and was a professional actress. Willie Morris has described the love affair–courtship in some detail.[63] It seems to have been funny and romantic and sometimes a little dangerous (Jones could not yet bring himself to break off with Lowney Handy). He proposed to Gloria in P. J. Clarke's, married her in Port-au-Prince, Haiti, February 27, 1957, and, after an unhappy and unsuccessful attempt to live in Jones's house in Marshall, they moved to New York in September of 1957. There Jones wrote *The Pistol* and finished it while they waited for the publication of *Some Came Running* on January 10, 1958. In April Jim and Gloria left for Europe planning to stay only awhile. But though they returned for many visits, they would not move back to the United States until the summer of 1974.

The marriage was a happy one, changed everything drastically for Jones, and lasted for the rest of Jones's lifetime. Willie Morris quotes Cecile Gray Bazelon, who was Gloria's roommate when she met Jones, as saying: "It was the beginning of the best single marriage I have ever known."[64]

In the more complex version, the next years, until he met and married Gloria and escaped to Europe, must have been some of the most difficult of his whole life. He was divided in several ways, and as time went on, the pressures on him acquired a brutal intensity.

A part of him wanted to enjoy the success of *Eternity* to the fullest and did so. He had ended a long period (actually going back to the time when he left for the Army with a couple of dollars in his pocket) of dependence, self-discipline, and deprivation. Now he had money to pay his debts and to contribute heavily to an idea he and the Handys had long planned—the Handy Artists Colony, of which he served as vice president. He now had the money to build a house and buy the things he wanted. He built an $85,000 house (designed by Harry Handy) of limestone and redwood, on an acre and a half in Marshall. Named for John Marshall, it is a rural, Wabash Valley town, with a population of about 3,000, and is set sixteen miles west of Terre Haute at an old and important crossroads, where the old Cumberland Road (running east–west, and the first road ever built with federal funds, during Jefferson's administration) meets the old stagecoach road, running north–south between Vincennes and Chicago. Marshall had known an early prosperity because of its location and the flour and woolen mills there. Later, from 1902 to 1916, there had been an oil boom. What was left of all that was a place with many fine old houses—and now a fine new one.

Aspects of Jones's house aroused some interest. Reporters loved to write it up while dealing with Jones's spectacular success story. Probably the most thorough piece on that period is Robert E. Cantwell's "James Jones: Another 'Eternity'?" in *Newsweek*. Writing about the house, he mentions that "a secret passageway has been completed to a secret chamber (purpose unannounced)."

Externally the house is a large, handsome, modified-modern, suburban dwelling, standing at the end of a secluded Marshall side street over-looking a large pasture and in the distance the county-fair grounds. Inwardly it is the sort of mansion that a man who has lived for years in a trailer might dream about. There is a huge living room, the full two stories high, in glass, brick and Philippine mahogany, but apart from that only a compact kitchen, combined sleeping and working quarters, a game room, and a bathroom that makes you think of something excavated from Pompeii.[65]

Shelby Foote remembers the house and the bathroom, too, from a visit there in the early 1950s. He recalls that there was "a gym and everything, even a two-toilet bathroom, his and hers, and a bidet, the only one in South Illinois."[66]

Within the house he was reported to have installed a $2,000 stereo system and to have on display a gun collection valued at $6,000. (He became a life member of the National Rifle Association.) He acquired projectors and movie-making equipment; he was learning to play chess and collecting chess sets; he was in touch with Bo Randall of Orlando, Florida, and buying Randall Made Knives, still thought by experts to be the best in the world; he was buying new books and rare books, American Indian jewelry in turquoise and silver, and Havana cigars. He began to collect rare coins, buying from Abner Kreisberg, numismatist of Los Angeles. He bought a trampoline from Nissen Corporation of Cedar Rapids. He bought a guitar and tried to learn the chords for "Rock Island Line." He was buying classical and jazz recordings, and he hired a musician in France to make copies of and send to him rare recordings of Django Reinhardt.

For outside he was investing in lawn-care tools, dealing with the Davy Tree Company to take care of his oaks and maples. Besides the jeep and the trailer, he now had a sports car, a Chrysler convertible, and a couple of motorcycles.

He bought clothes, favoring jeans and expensive cowboy shirts. He loved hats, too, but found it difficult to get ones that fit right—size 7¼ was too small and 7⅜ was a little too large.

When he went to New York for business and fun, he and friends hung out at Ratazzi's near Scribner's. And there was a literary group which gathered at the White Horse Tavern at the corner of 11th Street and Hudson. According to Hilary Mills in *Mailer: A Biography*, the informal group included Mailer and Jones and Styron, Vance Bourjaily and John Aldridge, Frederic Morton and (once) Hortense Calisher, Calder Willingham, John Marquand, Jr., and Mickey Knox, among others. It is to Knox that Mills attributes the story of William Styron pausing at a street corner, putting his arms around James Jones and Norman Mailer, and announcing: "Hey, fellas, isn't it wonderful? The three greatest young writers in America, and here we are together."[67]

Jones first met Montgomery Clift at a party in Greenwich Village at Vance Bourjaily's apartment. Even though Harry Cohn of Columbia wanted John Derek for the part of Prewitt, and Jones had originally wanted Zachary Scott, Jones decided that Clift was a better choice than either and promised to do what he could.[68] Supporting this version are several letters by Jones strongly urging people at Columbia, including the formidable Cohn, to use Clift in the part. These are followed by a letter of December 4, 1952, from Clift at the Hotel Hassler in Rome saying that he had gotten the part.[69]

A celebrity himself, Jones moved easily among other celebrities of all kinds, and not merely the movie and show business types. A number of people who knew Jones have made a good deal out of the pleasure he took in knowing the elite. In "Versions of Jones," Seymour Krim, himself a scholar of fame and the famous in America, describes Jones as possessing "something of the charisma of a heavyweight boxing champion." "There was something big and flashy about his tastes," Krim writes, "gambling, drinking, dining at the best places, hobnobbing with Frank Sinatra and Monty Clift etc.—that was unashamedly rank. . . . But beneath those trappings, Jones was private enough to be deeply disillusioned with the very materials of the world which he seemingly coveted."[70] But there are other sides to this frank enjoyment of socializing with the celebrated. One is that he seems invariably to have treated people the same, giving full attention and being charming, whether they were "important" or not. Richard Elman, then a young writer and virtually unknown, recalls meeting Jones at a party given by their mutual editor, Burroughs Mitchell. And to this day he has never forgotten the interested and considerate way he was treated by the older, well-known writer. It is a typical story, the irony of which is only this—that each time the teller of an anecdote or memory was somehow amazed to be treated as an equal by Jones.[71] It is pure speculation, but one may conclude that part of Jones's success with these people came precisely from his essentially democratic viewpoint. It may never have occurred to him that the famous were in any significant way different from anybody else. He seems to have treated celebrities like ordinary people and ordinary people like celebrities. With the result that they both loved it. In "James Jones: Another 'Eternity'?" Robert Cantwell casually mentions that Jones seems to have "a phobia about hurting other people's feelings." He adds: "Success, according to Jones, did not change him—other people changed."[72]

Above all, Jones had his fundamental innocence and simplicity to shield him from the worst wounds of success. He could enjoy it in a very simple, straightforward way. David Ray, who traveled with Jones from Tucson to join the Handy group at Marshall in 1954, recollects something pertinent about this:

> When a highway patrolman stopped us in Texas for speeding & for the trailer being too long (a 31 foot airstream as I recall), Jim was incredibly pleased because the guy recognized him as the famous writer James Jones and let him off without a ticket. Publicity for Jim was a big thing because he had gotten a lot, suddenly, & was aware of its corrupting potential. Lowney would warn him not to believe his publicity & he said "When you start believing your publicity you're in a lot of trouble" or would mention someone that he didn't like & say that was the trouble with him, that he believed his publicity. But Jim was very proud of knowing celebrities—Burt Lancaster, Monty Clift (very fond of him), and he was proud that he had slept with some movie star or starlet in Hollywood—at least he bragged about it.[73]

Which was all natural enough, even though it did not make his life any simpler.

After *Eternity* it was almost impossible for Jones to be anonymous. The press (*Newsweek, Life, Look, Pageant,* among others, plus various newspapers and columnists) did pieces on his success story. Some of them were acutely embarrassing, and all of them were part of a pattern of mounting pressure he had to contend with. To handle his increasingly complicated business affairs he now needed Horace Manges, the lawyer, and an accountant (Aaron Fuchs & Co.) and another lawyer, Kenneth B. Hawkins, to handle his problems in Illinois, especially those concerning the Handy Colony. There were various special legal problems. There was the problem of a James Jones impersonator, who popped up in California, then vanished without a trace. There was the problem of a Post Office obscenity case against *Eternity*—Case No. 4090-F. Details concerning this case are somewhat obscure at this point. Miscellaneous papers among the James Jones Archives of the Humanities Research Center indicate that Horace Manges handled the problem for Scribner's and for Jones. At the time Post Office regulations permitted the Post Office to forbid the use of the mails to materials judged to be obscene. Scribner's had feared this possibility all along (see page 94), but it appears that there was a regulatory hearing of this case on December 22, 1953, and that Horace Manges obtained a decision favorable to Scribner's and *Eternity*. A more serious problem, as far as Jones was concerned, had to do with a man in Brooklyn named Maggio who, it developed, had in fact served at the same time as Jones in F Company, 2nd Battalion, 27th Infantry Regiment at Schofield and on Gaudalcanal. Attended by considerable publicity, Maggio brought a civil suit for libel and invasion of privacy, basing his claim on Jones's treatment of the character Maggio in *Eternity*. This suit dragged on, unsettled, and finally went to litigation and trial by jury. It was settled in Jones's favor just before he left for Europe. There was no denying that he had used the real Maggio for a model, as he very often used real people as models for his fictional characters. As Jones explained it candidly to Manges in a letter of March 8, 1954: "I didn't portray his life, because everything that happened to him in the book did not happen to him in life. I didn't portray his personality either, I think, because I enlarged and purified it a great deal. I did describe him pretty much physically as he was then."[74] Jones told Manges that he had honestly believed Maggio was dead—killed in action in New Georgia. A letter from Jones to Mitchell supports Jones in this. In the letter Jones mentions running into an old buddy from F Company who was able to bring him up to date on people and things. "He said he heard Maggio got killed," Jones writes, "at Munda, New Georgia."[75]

Jones, who seems often to have used real people as starting points for his characters, was very careful after the drawn-out Maggio lawsuit. Among the papers at Texas are copies of various "release" forms, drawn up and signed by the living principals of *Go to the Widow-Maker*. Elsewhere, among the papers at Yale and Texas, are miscellaneous lists of people who *correspond to* characters in the later books. And there is at least one reference, which might well surprise scholars of modern literary history, concerning the character of Bob French, "minor poet" and professor in *Some Came Running*: "I decided to make Prof a distinctive minor poet, somewhat in the manner of John Crowe Ransom, who is related to the Revels of Flat Rock (12 miles from Robinson in our county)."[76]

The day that he received the news from Manges that he was being sued by Maggio was also the day he learned that Harry Brague, editor at Scribner's, had lost six chapters of the manuscript of *Running* by leaving them on the train. Fortunately Jones had another copy of the material. His answer to Mitchell tried to be more or less cheerful. "Well," he wrote, "Sunday was a big day. I got the letter from you about the lost chapters and at the same time a letter from Horace saying that Maggio had filed civil suit for $500,000 for both libel and right of privacy."[77]

The Handy Colony was constantly on his mind. (In more cheerful moods he called it "Ali Babble and the Farting Thieves.") It was an expensive enterprise and one that he wanted to make work. He felt that he owed it to Lowney Handy to help her realize this dream of hers. He put a great deal of his own money into it. Indeed, on June 20, 1953, he had his lawyer draw up a last will and testament naming the Handys as his beneficiaries. As a result of much effort on his part, and on the part of Lowney Handy, a number of people who had been associated with the small writers' group at one time or another managed to write books and to get them published: Edwin Daly, *Some Must Watch* (1956); Gerald Tesch (Jerry Tschappat), *Never the Same Again* (1956); and Tom Chamales, *Never So Few* (1957). Of these few, Chamales had considerable success with his novel and indeed had written and published a second book, *Go Naked in*

Jones with Montgomery Clift

On a lecture tour, late 1950s

With Cornelia Otis Skinner, 1962

the World (1959), when in March of 1960 he died in a house fire in Los Angeles. Chamales had, for a time, been a close friend of Jones, was his best man, and lent him $1,000 when he married Gloria. But Chamales and Jones were estranged by the time Jones moved to Paris. In 1961, Seymour Krim, then editor of *Nugget*, wrote to ask Jones if he would write a piece about Chamales. "I have large qualms," Jones replied. "There are so many bad things about Tom which would have to be said, and which I would not like to say but which must be said to get anything like a true picture, that I think the thing is better left untouched."[78]

In the end, when he broke with Lowney Handy, Jones would have to give up on the idea of the colony, but in those days he worked hard to keep it alive, often in the face of a good deal of negative or at least satirical publicity. Newspaper and magazine articles about Jones inevitably had to deal with the fact of the colony and with the theories of Lowney Handy, who was quoted in the lengthy *Newsweek* piece, "From Eternity to Here," as saying proudly, "I can teach anybody to write."[79] Her methods—manual labor, limited and low-protein diet, long periods of enforced silence, the copying out of assigned masterworks, and learning "writing in skits," combined with her own inimitable pastiche of occult and eastern philosophies —were certainly fair game for anyone with a healthy sense of skepticism. Even a sympathetic piece, like that of Marianne Besser (in spite of its eye-catching title), "Writers' Concentration Camp," in *Writers' Digest* (September 1955), made the place and its practices, not to mention Mrs. Handy herself with her large, burning brown eyes, sound bizarre in the extreme.[80]

Not all accounts were sympathetic, by any means. David Ray, now a poet and editor and one of the very few former members of the colony to establish for himself a lifetime career in literature, left college in Arizona to go to Illinois and join the colony with Jones and Mrs. Handy. For a while. After he left them, he wrote a number of pieces about the colony, from the inside, pieces which did nothing to endear him to Mrs. Handy. Probably the best known of Ray's articles is "Mrs. Handy's Writing Mill," in *London Magazine*.[81] There is also a combined review and exposé which appeared when *Some Came Running* was first published—"A Novel for Teacher," in *The Nation*:

A writer under her tutelage, for example, has no breakfast, "because you think better that way." He is also forbidden to talk until noon, because Mrs. Handy has adopted the Eastern conception of the creative value of silence. Her students must write steadily until noon, then devote the afternoon to penitent physical labor, carrying out her comparison of writers to monks. They must also undergo a period of "copying" verbatim on their typewriters various works (by Hemingway, Wolfe, Dos Passos, Raymond Chandler) that Mrs. Handy assigns. When employed on his own prose, the novice hands in what he has produced each day, and she goes over it with him, reinterpreting scenes or suggesting slants consistent with her views on psychology.[82]

But probably the most damaging and annoying piece by Ray came earlier in *Chicago* magazine (September 1956) : "The works of Marcel Prowst and Die-lane Thompson are verboten at MRS. HANDY'S CURIOUS COLONY : The author of *From Here to Eternity* and a number of less renowned writers inhabit a strange settlement downstate. A refugee tells of his experiences with this remarkable retreat, and its totally outlandish sponsor."[83] Jones was angry enough to write his Chicago lawyer to see if anything could or should be done about it.[84] It is not so much a matter of ridicule; for in spite of eccentric statements and theories, Lowney Handy emerges in the article as a powerful, even a potentially dangerous personality. Probably most irritating to·Jones was Ray's observation that the Handy method of "copying" seemed to be clearly demonstrated by parts of *From Here to Eternity*, because "certain passages in Jones' book appear almost identical not only in style but in content to parts of novels which he 'copied' on his typewriter for more than seven years." He proceeds to cite parallels to *Of Time and the River, The Naked and the Dead, U.S.A., The Great Gatsby,* and *For Whom the Bell Tolls.*[85]

In addition to the headaches associated with managing and defending the colony, Jones spent much energy carefully answering all the letters that poured in—not only the usual letters from his many real friends, nor mere fan mail and requests for autographs (which he usually responded to patiently), but also letters from writers wanting him to read unpublished manuscripts or to write blurbs for their books, queries of all kinds from students and academics and critics, requests for information and interviews from journalists. And, too, there were the letters that could not be answered, pathetic (true and false) requests for money, denunciatory letters from crazies attacking him for some aspect or another of *Eternity*. Some were merely insulting. "Your book, contrary to the critics' opinions, was terrible." Others were less temperate. "To my way of thinking," a letter begins, "I have never read anything as filthy, dirty, rotten, stinking, lousy and etc."

Not until later, in Paris, did Jones have a secretary to help him. At this point he tried to do it all himself.

And then there were family problems and in one case a tragedy. On June 5, 1952, Jones's sister Tink, who was the only woman Lowney Handy allowed to be a member of the colony, died there of some kind of seizure. She was found dead that morning, having evidently fallen out of her bunk in the night. The doctors listed the cause of her death as natural; but Jones's Uncle Charles, from whom Jones was, by then, bitterly estranged, seems to have believed in at least the possibility of some kind of "foul play." There is a letter concerning this from Jones to his Chicago lawyer (December 17, 1956),[86] but by then Charles Jones, too, was dead, killed in an automobile accident on Tuesday, December 4, 1956. Remembering his own youthful ineptitude at baseball and team sports, Jones must have winced at these sentences from Charles Jones's obituary in the *Robinson Argus*: "Mr. Jones had been long prominent in this county. When he was a young man he was an outstanding athlete and was an exceptionally good baseball player. Older residents will recall when he was catcher for the old Alpines and could usually be counted on for a long one over the fence when it was his turn at bat."[87]

Throughout this time, whether he was at home in Marshall or on the move, Jones was up every day by 5:30 A.M., working five or six hours on *Some Came Running*. Day after day, in spite of all pressures and distractions, this huge, enormously ambitious, difficult, and profoundly experimental work was growing. And he was strictly dedicated to it. David Ray recalls traveling with him, on a trip from Tucson, Arizona, to the writing colony in Marshall, Illinois, in 1954: "We'd stop at trailer parks, have a beer or 2 & dinner, play the pinball machines, turn in and read. I admired the austerity of Jim's life, actually, so don't warm to these images of him as a big party man. At that time he was very serious indeed, disciplined, informal in all things."[88]

Until he had completed the massive enterprise of *Some Came Running*, Jones did very little other writing during this period. He did some work, early on, for Hecht-Lancaster on a film script called "The Killing Frost," and in mid-1954 he seems to have tried his hand at some writing for

CBS Television. He attempted to assist a writer named Mark J. Appleman, who had written a stage version of the stockade sequence of *Eternity*. He at least considered a proposal to make a musical out of *Eternity*.[89] There were a couple of stories: "King," the story of a college jazz band, published in *Playboy* (October 1955); and "A Bottle of Cream," published in *New World Writing* 13. Both were to be included later in *Ice-Cream Headache*. There was the short piece on "Marshall, Ill." for *Ford Times* in 1957. And there were two relevant articles, specifically concerned with issues which were primary to the world of *Some Came Running*. "Living in a Trailer," appearing in the July 1952 issue of *Holiday*, came directly out of Jones's experience of moving across country from one trailer camp to the next. He celebrated and described a number of the camps he had stayed in. But, more to the point of *Running*, he described and praised America's itinerant blue-collar workers, a new class (coming out of an old one) created by the new mobility and by the wars, now including Korea:

> You can usually meet the labor group and their wives by going to the bar nearest the park and ordering a beer. They are a stiff, proud, independent bunch, used to travelling and inclined to be captious if you're wearing a white collar; otherwise they're friendly. If you're dressed in a T-shirt and levis, they like you—even if they know you're a writer. And if you admire crafts and skills you can't help but like them. Bricklayers, steelworkers, machinists, they follow defense work or construction jobs back and forth across the country.[90]

A little later in the same piece he accounts for the pleasures of this transient life as, in a sense, a kind of continuation of the soldier's life. "There is also, in a park," he wrote, "a curious sense of poignancy which is lent to trailer-camp life by the awareness that before long you'll be leaving. It's the same thing that makes a man's life seem more sparkling in a war, simply because he may shortly lose it."[91]

So much of what was happening in America in the 1950s may be attributed to the desire of millions of veterans, even as they consciously worked to shed memories of the war and habits of the armed forces like dead skin, to preserve this sense of life "sparkling." This is a fairly subtle observation, one which has been missed by many professional social critics. On one level Jones was extremely sensitive to what was happening in and to his country, and against huge odds, he tried to give it all coherence in his huge new novel.

However, Jones was not particularly sensitive to (or much interested in) some of the literary and intellectual directions of the 1950s. He was too busy to notice some of those matters and could not have been aware of how the ground (of literary tradition) was shifting underneath his feet. The postwar years, on through the 1950s, saw the triumph of the New Criticism, which on its simplest level, by its emphasis on the purity of text outside of any social context, made artistic sensitivity to that context something of an irrelevance. Secondly, by focusing such intense concentration upon text, in abstraction from other considerations, it inevitably made *style*, and primarily authorial style as distinct from narrative style, the most important element in poetry and fiction. Jones's fiction, designed according to another set of rules and other criteria, simply cannot stand up to the particular kind of scrutiny which the New Critics wished to enforce. He would be in for a beating from that crowd, as Robie Macauley's *Kenyon* review of *Eternity* should have warned him. Moreover Jones, as he wrote *Running*, was involved in an experiment with language, a kind of discovery. He speaks of this most fully in a *Paris Review* interview. He calls it working with "colloquial forms,"[92] by which he means not merely the free and easy use of the living, *spoken* American idiom in dialogue or in first-person narration, but the attempt to carry it into the narrative itself, into third-person narrative. This means, without being unduly technical, that not only are the thoughts and words of the characters presented appropriately in the vernacular, but also much of the narrative itself, as if the author-narrator were speaking almost in a composite language of the characters, within the context of the characters' own verbal capacities and limitations. In a variety of forms this experimental concern of what to do with the rapidly changing American vernacular, particularly in dealing with characters whose verbal abilities were either limited or, at the least, not conventionally *literary* (in the sense that even a well-read doctor or lawyer may use a different kind of language from that of a critic or professor), troubled and engaged many of the best American writers during the same period, for instance William Faulkner, Wright Morris, John O'Hara, Calder Willingham, and James Gould Cozzens. Cozzens was crucified by critics precisely for the triumph of his "colloquial forms" in *By Love Possessed*. Faulkner was often chastised—and the opinions of his characters were attributed to him—even for *first-person* use of vernacular variety. If the critics were not able to handle first-person narration without confusion, despite the absolutely correct decorum of Arthur Winner in *By Love Possessed*—and they could not, being, by and large, unable or unwilling to recognize what Cozzens was trying to do—how could they possibly have appreciated Jones's snarled narrative style as he tried to dramatize the difficulties of the people and classes in the dying American heartland in their own honest speech?

But there was yet another factor working against Jones in those years. And this was probably beyond Jones's imagination, because like most self-educated men, he trusted and respected intellectuals. He was not able to conceive that those who professed the humanities, who had given their lives to the cultivation of ideas in a society which seemed devoted to material things, that people such as these could also be petty, small-minded, mean of spirit, fearful, and fearfully ambitious. If (as they did) the New Critics represented the social and political American right, the urban intellectual critics came out of the traditions of the European left. The war in Korea, the Cold War, the booming Eisenhower years, the ragings of Senator Joseph R. McCarthy and the House Un-American Affairs Committee, brought the left together as they had not been before and would not be again. In that sense Joe McCarthy was the best friend the American left ever had. The evidence has accumulated from many sources and most recently from the books of memoirs by active participants—books like William Barrett's *The Truants* and Irving Howe's *A Margin of Hope* among many others—that in that time of perceived danger, the left dug in strongly and defensively (well-protected, of course, by the Bill of Rights). And the left, though it might indulge in some minor family quarrels, could allow for no middle ground and certainly viewed culture, the arts, not as peripheral to the class struggle, but as a cutting edge in an ideological war. Control and discipline were essential if the left were to survive. Add to this an ethnic distinction. Though Americans, old and new, overwhelmingly supported the quiet social revolution of the New Deal years and now at least tacitly tolerated the social revolution being accomplished in the 1950s by the Warren Court, nevertheless the younger generations of Americans felt closer to the non-Anglo-Saxon European traditions of political action than to the American. The paradoxes and contradictions of Thomas Jefferson (or Andrew Jackson) were more exotic to them than those of Karl Marx or Leon Trotsky.

Thus, by the time that *Some Came Running* was finished and ap-

Jones's sister, Mary Ann, as a young woman

Shirley MacLaine and Frank Sinatra in Some Came Running

peared, both Jones, as the natural heir of the old, middle-American, democratic-populist tradition, and his *subject*, the impact of the war and modernity upon the rigidities of a middle-American town, stood in contradiction to the intellectual establishment in just about every imaginable way. True, he had shown a certain naive potentiality for leftist ideology in some parts of *Eternity*, and certainly a blow against the Army could be taken as a blow against Fascism; but in the years between the two books, middle America, indeed all of America outside of the preserves of the eastern seaboard and the coastal pale of California, had become foreign territory, the enemy of the intellectual establishment. Perhaps Eisenhower's overwhelming election victories had triggered the process. In any case, during the 1950s the American intellectual establishment lost faith and interest in the American people. And if the left could not win power at the ballot box, it could at least exercise great power, and often have the last word—from the security of the elite academies—over what, in our time, has come to be called the media. Prescient and sensitive as he was, Jones, like most middle Americans, still could not have imagined that such things were coming to pass. In *Some Came Running* he was plainly worried about hypocrisy and corruption, about parallels between postwar America and declining ancient Rome. He sensed that things were falling apart and that many good things were dying along with expendable, indeed unworthy old ways; but naively he imagined all men of goodwill were more or less on the same side, wishing the best for each other and the nation and the world.

But it was, in fact, intellectual war. And Jones, like Cozzens and Faulkner and O'Hara and many others, even Farrell, was on the wrong side, an enemy. I recall from that period hearing a prominent magazine editor, *still* a prominent magazine editor as I write this, saying with pride that he had recently rejected work submitted by Nobel Prize–winner William Faulkner, not on the grounds of quality but rather, as he saw it, as a small contribution to the civil rights movement. Jones was up against that kind of thinking. Jones's sense of what was happening to America was not really ideological, but it was accurate and honest enough to annoy ideological purists of several persuasions.

In "Too Much Symbolism," the second important article written by Jones during this period, one which is directly concerned with issues raised in *Some Came Running*, Jones was replying to a query about "values." First of all, he saw the present situation as two-sided:

There is a lot in our age today that is similar to the Elizabethan age, I think. [Gloria Jones reports that Jones had a lifetime fascination with all things Elizabethan.] The unrest, the perpetual wars, the opening up of new scientific and spatial frontiers, the sense of living daily amid many great dangers to continued existence. Individual life is growing much cheaper in our country—just as well as the rest of the world—no matter how loud we Americans holler the opposite; and on the other side of the same coin, the hidden side, the average person is living with much greater vitality than we usually admit, simply because he is existing under such stress.[93]

Ideologues were not interested in thinking about "the other side of the same coin, the hidden side."

Jones also seemed to sense the growing separation between the American intellectual class and other people. The intellectuals did not want to be *like other people*. He saw it in the increasing separation of the *writer*, including himself, from the facts of life, from the concerns of people, and from the texture of experience.

I think one result of this attitude of ours is that we find ourselves concerned more with symbolism than with characters. Thus instead of letting our characters write our books we let our ideas write our characters. . . . We worry about values. Have writers lost their values? Has our culture lost its values? Are there any values left anywhere? Meantime, the people who don't read our books and don't know themselves to be valueless go right on living as if they valued things.[94]

Jones had an intense awareness of the advance, like an infectious disease, of corruption into many aspects of American life. But Jones does not seem to have imagined that the intellectual community, and in particular the critics, were to be as easily infected as anybody else. Critics may not have traded favors for vicuña coats, but they were perfectly willing to play follow-the-leader with new books as they came along. And the fact that they had not actually read a book they were reviewing, especially a very long book like *Some Came Running*, did not awaken conscience enough for them to disqualify themselves from passing judgment.

Jones finished the task of *Some Came Running* in 1956. Near the end of it he would write Mitchell, "I'm running on a pretty thin ragged edge to get this done. . . ."⁹⁵ He and Mitchell cut the manuscript, hacking away large chunks—though, as they agreed later, probably not nearly enough. By December 16, 1956, Jones was already able to write Mitchell his plan to do a new version of "They Shall Inherit the Laughter" as his next book. In this letter it sounds very much like *Whistle*. Jones had all kinds of plans for the future. As he had written Norman Mailer: "You know, old buddy, I feel as if I were just beginning to come into the richest and most productive and most mature period of my life. I want to take full advantage of it. I want to stay right here for the next ten to fifteen years and get a bulk of good work done that will assure me a real place."⁹⁶

He was to get much work done in the years ahead. But it was *not* the future he imagined then. For in early 1957, the best thing that had ever happened to Jones came to pass. He was staying at the Olafson Hotel with Gloria Mosolino. On February 27, 1957, he put on a brand new, white Palm Beach suit. Gloria wore white lace. A black Haitian judge, Pere Duncan, made them man and wife under the Napoleonic Code.

Once he saw that Marshall, Illinois, would not suit him and Gloria, he drove off without looking back.

Some Came Running is a huge novel, running, in its unabridged hardcover edition, more than twelve hundred pages in fine print. It is richly decorated with a wealth of literary epigraphs—Sir Walter Raleigh, Cervantes, Edna St. Vincent Millay, the Bible. It opens with a poignant dedication to the memory of his dead sister. The story is bracketed between a complex and somewhat sarcastic Special Note in the front and a personal Acknowledgement at the end. These devices tend to distance the story and to focus attention on the author. The actual narrative is set between a Prologue, concerned with combat action in the Battle of the Bulge, and an Epilogue dealing with combat and brutal death in Korea. It offers an enormously detailed, and frequently digressive account of life in Middle America, specifically in the imaginary town of Parkman, Illinois, in the years between World War II and Korea, with a large cast of deeply troubled characters of various backgrounds and ages. Most, civilians as well as veterans, have been crippled by the experience of World War II. The point of view is omniscient, permitting the narrator and the reader to see things from many sides and to enter into the consciousness of any character; but the story is, nonetheless, built primarily around the life, tough times, and sudden death of Dave Hirsh, a thirty-six-year-old ex-G.I., a writer and a native of Parkman who has not returned home in nineteen years. There are numerous other significant characters: the literary virgin Gwen French, whom Dave loves and lusts for but does not win; her father, a professor and minor poet; the restless southerner and professional gambler 'Bama Dillert; Dave's brother Frank, a model of local rectitude and hypocrisy; Ginnie Moorhouse, the mill girl whom Dave marries for all the wrong reasons; Jane Staley, perhaps best described as a triumphantly dirty old lady. It is by and through the gradual revelations of character and of their conceptions and misconceptions of each other that the story is told. These people are only, at best, partly successful at understanding each other. And they are even less able to comprehend honestly their own motives. Such a story needs space to develop, because all of the characters are so mixed, deeply ambivalent, and self-deceiving even as they seek to deceive others. That they are all sometimes as silly and foolish as they are misguided or wicked makes the story as funny as it is bitter. To the conventional state of hypocrisy in small-town American life, Jones has added a wealth of sexual confusion and self-delusion. When *Running* appeared, *Peyton Place*, that seething caldron of sex in small-town America, had been on the best-seller list for months; but Jones was interested in depicting much more than commonplace sexual hypocrisy. His characters are sexual grotesques; each is lost and lonely, hopelessly confused in the search for a sexual identity. Moreover, in a larger sense, the whole nation is depicted in a state of confusion, torn between decaying old values and new ways of life.

This situation is perceived as parallel to the rise and fall of ancient Rome.

Much of the story is told through dialogue, a direct form of dramatization virtually necessitated by the split between theory and practice in the lives of all the characters. If theory is false, then the theory must be fully expounded to make that point. Distinction between narration and dialogue is minimized by the use of "colloquial forms." The result of all this is an enormously complex and demanding book, one which requires patient and intense concentration for the reader not to fall into some of the misconceptions that bedevil the characters. It would be a mistake, at any point, to attribute any of the characters' opinions, theories, prejudices, and follies to the author. But it is an easy mistake to make; and a great many readers, starting with most of the reviewers, seem to have done so. Though some of the characters share some ideas and notions with the author, not one can stand, even briefly, as a mouthpiece for Jones. Neither here, nor, as far as I can tell, in any of the other novels. The relationship of Jones to his fictional characters is more complex than he has often been given credit for.

Yet in spite of its unquestionable honesty, its humor, and the gritty specificity of much of the story, the novel, taken in its own terms, is a bleak one and can be interpreted as a dark picture of the future of the American dream. Thus, not without real courage, the popular and successful writer, James Jones, produced a very different book from what might have been expected, a difficult book about very unhappy people. What was original was easy to miss. What was admirable was easy to ignore.

Some Came Running appeared and was immediately ambushed by an army of critics. Even a considerate review, like that of David Dempsey in the *New York Times Book Review*, which found some things to praise, couldn't resist indulging in a pun, calling the work "a relentless and often tedious *seductio ad absurdum*."[97] Others went for the solar plexus. Here is Edmund Fuller in the *Chicago Sunday Tribune*: "If you like bad grammar, it is there, as much in the narrative as in the dialog. If you like the grossest promiscuity, the most callous adultery, aggressive vulgarity, shoddy and befuddled philosophy, 'Some Came Running' is your book."[98] *Time* named Jones as "the Stanley Kowalski of U.S. letters" and described the book, "at its frequent worst," as "a mishmash of joyless fornication, head-splitting hangovers, and neo-Dreiserian conviction that life itself is a four-letter word."[99] Here is how the *Library Journal* lowered the boom: "This is a 1200 page orgy of sex, self-pity and sloppy prose and it will be a long time before the reader will forget the hours lost ploughing through Jones' murky writing."[100] *The New Yorker* called the book "Twelve hundred and sixty-six pages of flawlessly sustained tedium, dealing with three years (1947–1950) in the lives of a handful of middle- and lower-class freaks. . . ." Adding that "the dominant and inescapable tone is that of Mr. Jones' own smudged, freshman prose."[101] *Commonweal*'s review defined the central characteristic of the book as "logorrhea compounded by editorial torpor, or editorial despair."[102] Charles Rolo, writing in *Atlantic*, called the novel "an outsize example of the hick novel," identifying Jones as "an essentially primitive mind" and describing his prose as characterized by "a drabness as dispiriting as the 'eats' on the counter of a sleazy beanery." Comparing the second novel with the first, which he had admired, Rolo wrote: "The savage passion which energized *From Here to Eternity* is muffled, and there remains the grammar of self-pity, to which is now added the earnest drone of portentous banalities."[103] And probably the most thorough workout came at the hands of the influential Granville Hicks in his "Living with Books" column in *The New Leader* where even the title— "James Jones's 'Some Came Running': A Study in Arrogant Primitivism" —was altogether bad news. Hicks deals at length with "the badness of the writing" arguing: "This is not just inept or careless writing, it is an assault upon the language." Arriving at the conclusion that what "one feels in Jones is not merely ignorance but also sheer hatred of the language." Judging: "I believe he is incapable of realizing just how gross, slovenly, and tasteless the book is, but if he could realize it I don't think he would care."[104]

Some Came Running found a place on the *Times*'s best-seller list, arriving at the eleventh spot on January 26, 1958. It was a list that included, in the number one position, Cozzens' *By Love Possessed*, plus such titles as *Atlas Shrugged*, *A Death in the Family*, *Last Tales* by Isak Dinesen, *The Fall* by Camus, William Humphrey's *Home from the Hill*, and also *Peyton Place* which, then in thirteenth place, had been on the list for sixty-eight weeks. *Some Came Running* was on the list for thirteen weeks, climbing highest on February 2 when it was in fourth place. Paperback rights were sold to New American Library for $50,000, though— unfortunately, as far as Jones was concerned—the contract stipulated that the paperback version would be an abridgment of the hardcover edition by some 50 to 60 percent. Film rights were sold to MGM for a tidy quarter of a million dollars, although that was not nearly as much as Jones had once hoped for.[105] It was produced and released in 1958. Directed by Vincente Minnelli (who also directed the 1958 film adaptation of *Home from the Hill*), it starred Frank Sinatra as Dave Hirsh, Shirley MacLaine as Ginnie, and Dean Martin as 'Bama Dillert. The only thing Jones liked about the picture was Martin's performance.[106]

But by April of 1958 he and Gloria had sailed to Europe.

Now that the dust has settled on the critical controversy about *Some Came Running*, there are a few things still left to be said. Willie Morris says one of them in *James Jones* when he singles out the long digressive sequence where 'Bama Dillert takes Dave Hirsh with him, driving the long road to the South and back. He describes this sequence as "stunningly truthful." "It was written," Morris says, "by a man who had done a lot of driving, and who knew the Great American Road."[107] Poet Kenneth Rosen, who came to the book without knowledge of it or any preconceptions, liked it enormously for its portrait of the factory girls—the young women in America who had come to the factories in World War II and never left them afterward. "Nobody else has really written much about those women," Rosen says.[108] Writing for the reference book, *Contemporary Novelists*, David Sanders puts *Some Came Running* in some perspective: "Very few people acknowledged that Jones was trying to write a more difficult book or that he had become a more complicated person in six more years of learning how to write."[109]

As for Jones, he bore his disappointment with dignity. He would sometimes need practice in dignified indifference in the years ahead. Maybe he was able to do so because he had already learned a great lesson while writing his second novel. In a piece not published until October 1976 in *Writers' Digest*, "Me and Mr. Jones," Lee Butcher, who was a young boy in Marshall in the 1950s, tells about a pleasant encounter he had with Jones when he went to Jones's house to return a jacket for his father, who happened to be chief of police. Butcher says Jones told him this, a thought which stayed with him.

"Don't practice the things that are easy for you," Jones told him. "Practice the hard things until they become easy, then go on to something harder. That's the way to grow."[110]

In New York while waiting for *Some Came Running* to come along, and dealing with the Maggio lawsuit, Jones kept busy by writing *The Pistol*, a complete change of pace. A short tight novel of roughly 150 pages, *The Pistol* (1959) focuses on one particular situation involving one particular character. His protagonist is a soldier at Schofield Barracks who (like Jones himself) happens to be an orderly on guard duty at the time of the attack on Pearl Harbor. Like Jones he is armed that day with a pistol, which, in the confusion of events, is overlooked, perhaps forgotten by the supply sergeant. The rest of the story, closely paralleling the experiences of Jones's company at Makapuu Head, concerns his attempt somehow to keep the pistol for himself, against all the odds, and against the envy and machinations of everyone else in the outfit. It becomes a matter of life and death to him. In the end, after a painful series of deceptions and self-deceptions, he fails. The pistol, at first an obsession and finally his whole reason for being, is routinely reclaimed by the system. The style is impersonal and understated. The story is pared to bare bones.

His protagonist, Pfc. Richard Mast—later to reappear as Pfc. Doll in *The Thin Red Line*—was originally called Richard Coon until Decherd Turner of the *Dallas Times-Herald*, who had previously reviewed Jones's work favorably, saw it in galley proof and called Jones's attention to the perhaps unfortunate and unintended connotations of that character name. Jones immediately changed it and had to hurry to catch the British edition, already in page proof.

The Pistol, published exactly one year after *Running*, is at once a highly successful piece of straightforward fiction and a virtuoso exercise, demonstrative proof that Jones could write a coolly conceived, condensed, and highly objective novel. It is a fine, clean story and an easy one to like. Jones had the bitter pleasure of seeing the critical response flip-flop from the negativism which had greeted *Some Came Running*. He would have read Granville Hicks in the *Saturday Review*, where Hicks concluded that *The Pistol* was "a good book" and used it to ask a serious question: "Does it [*The Pistol*] indicate a change of heart, or did Jones write it just to show that he can be a disciplined writer if he sets out to be?"[111]

By and large *The Pistol* received favorable reviews, though there were a few attacks on it like that of William James Smith in *The Commonweal*. Warming to his task, Smith wrote: "Never has one man said so few things so many times in so brief an expanse." He added, in final judgment: "It is no more than an intolerably drawn-out 'incident,' hoked up with a little spurious 'simplicity' to look as though it meant something."[112] Jones himself seems to have had mixed feelings about *The Pistol*. He did not choose to include it in his grand design for a World War II novel (which became the trilogy), even though, in fact, it fits perfectly. He seems consistently to have refused to consider *The Pistol* as belonging among his major works.[113]

*Inside every fat drunk there is another drunk
who believes he's skinny.*

James Jones[1]

*Eventually the house [Scribner's] is going to
have to pull itself out of the 19th century or
else it will get lost completely, or become just
a textbook publisher. I don't say I like
mid-twentieth century methods or ethics. But
in our era that is what works and therefore
what one has to do to survive.*

James Jones[2]

PART FOUR
• • •
PARIS YEARS

·   ·   ·

FROM April to August of 1958 the Joneses lived in London, first at the Stafford Hotel, then in a flat at 61 Eaton Place. Jones had begun work on *The Thin Red Line*. In spite of the fact that they had good friends in London, they moved on to Paris. It seemed that they were still looking around, not ready to settle down permanently anywhere. Enchanted with the city, but not yet imagining it would be their home for years to come, they rented an apartment on the Quai aux Fleurs.

The Paris years . . . really, the years of residence there, for the Joneses traveled widely in Europe and the Caribbean during that time and regularly returned to the United States for business and visits, though these American visits had to be of strictly limited duration in order for them to maintain legal residence in Paris and to take advantage of tax laws. The Paris years were such *fun*. They were fun to write about, and over the years a number of excellent pieces have dealt with Jones in Paris. Probably the definitive treatment is in Willie Morris' *James Jones: A Friendship*.[3]

But there were other sympathetic and interesting articles. Most were written at the time during which the Joneses' enlarged, restored, refurbished, and altogether remarkable apartment on the Île Saint Louis (10, Quai d'Orléans; phone: DAN 1850) was a busy social center, a kind of informal and unofficial American embassy for large numbers of stray literati and ordinary traveling Americans. *Life* magazine had always found Jones good copy, and Hugh Moffett wrote a sympathetic piece, "Aging Heavy of the Paris Expatriates," for the August 4, 1967, issue. "America has not seen this remarkable U.S. literary figure for a decade," he wrote. "He is a rich, successful author nursing his young man's literary anger into a middle age which in contrast has seemed to make him mellow and sensitive." Moffett describes the Sunday night spaghetti, whiskey, and poker evenings as "the most stimulating place for an artist or writer to be"; he tells of such soon-to-be-legendary features as the sixteenth century pulpit Jones had made into a bar, the spiral staircase, the bathroom with synthetic leopard skin for wallpaper, the extensive collections of contemporary paintings and sculpture, of beer steins and cowboy outfits. Moffett makes the point that Jones was still working hard, four or five hours every day at a huge antique desk, although he might start in a little late, as late as 10:00 A.M. "if it has been a rough night."[4] He mentions Jones's steady vice—good cigars; how Jones allowed himself seven two-dollar Cuban cigars a day; how he spent $420 a month on cigars. He did not mention—perhaps because he did not notice it—that by that date Jones was drinking nothing but a little white wine and that he was doing his best to stick to a bland and nearly salt-free diet. Gloria Jones remarks that he managed his self-discipline so gracefully that very few people noticed it when he didn't drink hard liquor with the others or when he passed up some example of good French gourmet cooking for something less rich.

A year later Jones's familiar face appeared in a photo in quite another sort of magazine—*The National Geographic*. Kenneth MacLeish's title, "Île de la Cité, Birthplace of Paris," is somewhat deceptive, for in the piece he deals with the neighboring Île St.-Louis, as well although, as MacLeish points out, Jones is associated with both islands. The very first apartment Jones and Gloria had, before they became *Louisiens*, was a small one above a little grocery store on the Île de la Cité (17, Quai aux Fleurs). They bought the larger apartment in 1960 when Gloria was pregnant, and they would soon need more room. MacLeish stresses Jones's enthusiasm for

Île St.-Louis and his appreciation of its special qualities. "There's nothing like it," he quotes Jones as saying. "Quiet. Great people. The shopping street's like a village market. You ought to see the fish store after dark. It's like a painting." He also makes something out of Jones's interest in the traditional *clochards* of Paris. "In summer the *clochards* like to live along the quai, sleep under the bridges," Jones says. "They keep pretty clean, too. Wash their underwear in the river. I was on the bum once, when I was a kid. You can learn a lot. . . ."[5]

By 1969, with Jones busy finishing a novel about Americans in Paris, Arthur Goodfriend produced an in-depth picture of Jones in Paris, part essay and part interview, for the *Saturday Review*.[6] Jones talked about why he had come to live in Paris and how he had managed to make a living there; the latter, Jones admitted, despite good publishing contracts and steady productivity, mostly by writing movie scripts:

I don't like writing movie scripts, but the pay is high and so is the price of Paris. My wife and I had come to Paris in 1958—we figured maybe for a year—but Gloria got pregnant and we had our choice of staying or going back to Pottsville, Pennsylvania. I was walking on the Île St.-Louis and saw a house with two floors for sale. The price was so steep, paying it off committed us to Paris for ten years. We flipped a coin and bought one floor. When our daughter Kaylie was born we needed more room. I put in my suit from Sills in New York, with no pads in the shoulders, carried a briefcase rattlingly empty except for a movie script, and went over to the Champs Élysées to see the producers, actors, and agents who hang out at Fouquets.

Well, today we own two floors with a Zanuck suite, a Mirisch suite, a Nicholas Ray suite, and I am scripting my way up to the third. As our bills get bigger, our roots grow deeper; Paris has become our home.[7]

The bills were getting bigger all the time. Some financial notes among the papers at the Humanities Research Center list the living expenses of the Jones family for 1970 as $149,691.

A good deal remains to be clarified concerning Jones's work for films. From notes and documents at Texas we know that in the summer and fall of 1961 he was working on both bits of dialogue and characterization for

The Joneses, the Styrons, and the Shaws, Paris, 1968

OPPOSITE: *Janet Flanner, Jones, Thornton Wilder, and Alice B. Toklas, Paris, 1959*   (Centre Culturel Américain)

OPPOSITE BOTTOM: *With Gloria at Deux Magots, Paris, 1960s*

View across the Seine from Paris apartment at 10 quai D'Orléans

Talking with Darryl Zanuck on the set of
The Longest Day

With Peter Lawford on location in France for
The Longest Day

Darryl F. Zanuck's *The Longest Day*, for which Zanuck paid him at least $10,000 (probably a good deal more). Likewise, under an agreement dated December 27, 1963, there appears to have been a full-scale treatment for the Mirisch Corporation of an adaptation of Joseph Conrad's *Under Western Eyes*. In 1969 Jones was evidently seeking permission to publish this treatment in book form, but nothing came of that. He had been unable at first to work out a sale of *The Pistol* to the movies, although there seems to have been some interest. As early as August 1, 1958, he wrote to Mitchell about interest shown by Irving Allen of Warwick Pictures. Gloria Jones reports that Jones eventually sold *The Pistol* to Allen for $50,000. It was never produced.

Although combat does figure in specific scenes—or at least in the memories of characters—in other Jones novels, *The Thin Red Line* (1962) is the only book he wrote which is exclusively devoted to warfare. It is his combat novel and the center of his World War II trilogy.

The Thin Red Line follows the men of an infantry unit, C-for-Charlie Company, from their arrival in Guadalcanal through two battles and the end of that campaign. In a Special Note Jones asserted that though he has placed the story in a real place, Guadalcanal, "I have taken the liberty of distorting the campaign and laying down smack in the middle of it a whole slab of nonexistent territory."[8] Whatever his good reasons for saying this, the statement is not precisely true. The terrain in the novel is almost identical to that faced by Jones's own F Company in 1943. And the events of the novel, down to the smallest of details, so closely follow the actual action of Jones's company—as this has gradually emerged in published histories of the campaign—as to give the book almost the quality of a nonfiction documentary. And this was the very quality Jones was seeking to create *technically* with the novel. The point of view is omniscient and constantly shifts from one character to another, touching briefly on many men rather than developing a few in depth. Some few are, inevitably, given more weight and space than others. In accord with the broader design of his planned World War II trilogy of novels, several of the characters, though given different names, have essentially the same characteristics as the principal figures in *From Here to Eternity*. These are key people in the Company: Warden becomes M/Sgt. "Mad" Welsh; Stark is now Mess Sergeant Storm; Private Witt is a version of the tragic Prewitt. And the young clerk, Corporal Geoffrey Fife, seems to be, among other things, a stand-in for James Jones, for many things which happened to Jones happen to him. Yet, deliberately, no one character is developed enough to take over the story. For it is the story of the company itself, whose being and character, whose very survival, in victory or defeat, is derived from the swallowing up of all the egos and individuality of everyone in the outfit. Jones uses this multifaceted narrative point of view coupled with a flat, impersonal style as a technique to underscore a major point of the novel: that modern warfare is not an individual affair except very rarely, very briefly and deceptively. Modern war becomes, as does the experience of the book itself, ruthlessly impersonal, indifferent equally to anguish and exaltation. There were a couple of other theoretical points, ideas enforced by his experience of combat, which Jones was able to embody pragmatically in this narrative technique. First of all, there is no such thing as rational cause and effect, except insofar as individual characters, themselves mere fragments, insist on perceiving some kind of order in chaos. In fact, from an individual point of view, there is only accident, pure luck, good or bad. Men and women live by accident and die by accident. Nothing they plan or do really makes any difference at all. Corresponding with this view is Jones's demonstration that each of these characters is constantly changing —cowardly one minute, brave the next, without rhyme or reason, as if they were being inwardly swept and mastered by the same sorts of accidental forces that dominate the field of battle. Some heroic things are done in *The Thin Red Line*, but there are no heroes.

In his *Paris Review* interview, given while *The Thin Red Line* was still in the works, Jones was explicit about his intention, above all, to tell the truth about the experience of combat: "I don't think that combat has ever been written about truthfully; it has been described in terms of bravery and cowardice. I won't even accept these words as terms of human reference any more. And, anyway, hell, they don't even apply to what, in actual fact, modern warfare has become."[9]

The novel is a remarkable technical achievement, but perhaps even more remarkable is that this hard, unflinching truth telling succeeded, that the book was generally very well received by reviewers and readers.

On the whole, good notices had greeted the appearance of *The Pistol*, but the reviews of *The Thin Red Line* were exceptionally fine and prominently featured in key publications. In the *New York Herald Tribune* book review Lewis Gannett called it as good as *Eternity*, adding that there were new dimensions, for Jones had "continued to grow." "But there is also a deeper understanding of the human condition of men in war," Gannett wrote, "and of the weird patterns of pride, avarice and accident which create what go down in the records as 'bravery' or 'cowardice.' "[10] In the front page review for *The New York Times* Book Review Maxwell Geismar wrote a rave review beginning with the statement that Jones "has kept his integrity, his own version of life. And he proves his talent and integrity once again with 'The Thin Red Line'."[11] Saul Bellow praised the book;[12] Norman Mailer gave it a complex and mixed report, but said that it was "so broad and true a portrait of combat that it could be used as a textbook in the Infantry School if the Army is any less chicken than it used to be."[13] (Years later, in his study *War and the Novelist*, Peter G. Jones could make this claim without anticipating contradiction: "As a fictional account of combat it is unsurpassed.")[14] Terry Southern reviewed it for *The Nation*, and his review could not have been more satisfactory or useful to the author, for it praised the book highly and also described the innovative qualities of the technique with great accuracy: "This is surely one of the strongest and most effective war novels ever written; even its immense length and Jones's habit, or method, if it is that, of redundance . . . work to advantage, suggesting the insane confusion, tedium and the endlessness of war. And there is behind the work a new kind of narrative; it is the 'omniscient author' taken toward a logical extreme, where the narration itself, although faceless, without personality, expresses feelings, both of individuals and collectively, in their own terms."[15]

This kind of sympathy and understanding may have led Jones to believe that, at last, as far as the critics were concerned, he had turned a corner, that nothing quite as harsh as the treatment of *Some Came Running* would come his way again. And in one sense that proved true, for in general nothing quite as bad as the reception of *Running* would be repeated. After *Thin Red Line* he would always earn mixed reviews, that is, at least some reviewers found things to like about what he wrote. But individual critics found ways to wound every time he published a book.

Thin Red Line was sold to film producer Philip Yordan and ultimately made and released in June of 1964, starring Keir Dullea. The first draft of the screenplay was written by British novelist Jon Manchip White who, as an enlisted man in the famed Welsh Guards of the Brigade of Guards, had seen a great deal of combat in World War II, far more than Jones. White liked Jones a lot, as a fellow Welshman ("He reminded me of the typical Welsh coalminer. I felt at home with him, that I knew him well. . . ."), but he did not like the novel very much.[16] Nor did he like what Yordan and others did to the script—changes in the original story that included adding an extensive dream sequence, "the whole point of which," *Newsweek*'s critic wrote, "seems to be merely to introduce Merlyn Yordan, wife of Philip Yordan"[17]—and so White had his name withdrawn from it. News of what was happening to the film version of *Line* during production in Spain reached Jones, but he seems not to have cared much what they did with it. "That doesn't bother me as long as I can be sure to make us money," he wrote to Mitchell on November 1, 1963.[18] Earlier he reported to Mitchell that he was working on "a western movie with Nick Ray, just for the money."[19] And October 29, 1963, he referred to *two* westerns he was involved with.[20]

It is just as well nobody worried about the fate of *The Thin Red Line* on the silver screen. For it was roughly handled by the film critics, especially the added dream sequence material introducing a female character into the context of what had been a lean, spare, coldly objective combat novel. As the *Newsweek* critic continued: "Of the scant beauties of Mrs. Yordan's person, the only possible gallantry is silence. Dullea's dream of her and home makes war seem not so bad."[21]

It was at this time that Jones began the process which would end with his leaving his old publisher, Charles Scribner's Sons. Looking back through the Scribner's files at Princeton and the papers and letters at Yale and Texas, one can, with the clarity of hindsight, see it coming, or see, anyway, the little clouds before they darkened and grew. Jones's sense of gratitude and loyalty was so strong that it required an equally strong inducement to allow him to set himself free. There had been some minor problems and aggravations all along, and they were exacerbated by such things as his justifiable feeling that *Some Came Running* could have been better handled—better presented and promoted by the publisher, who had also sold the paperback rights for less than half of what *Eternity* had brought and under a humiliating contract which permitted New American Library to use the radical surgery of extensive abridgment. *The Pistol*, despite some well-placed, favorable reviews, had not done nearly as well as he had hoped it would, and Scribner's had sold the paperback rights for an advance of only $17,000 (of which his share was half).

The Thin Red Line had done quite well for Jones (and Scribner's) in a number of ways. The original contract, calling for a December 1, 1961, delivery date, though it offered no advance (by Jones's choice, apparently for tax reasons), gave him a beginning royalty rate of 15 percent. The book was taken by the Book-of-the-Month Club as an alternate, sold to New American Library for an advance of $75,000, and the reprint contract called for royalties to be divided, after sale of the first 100,000 copies, at a ratio of 60/40 in Jones's favor. The book sold well, taking its place on the best-seller list. But there were misunderstandings. Jones was under the impression that after the sale of 50,000 copies (and by January 14, 1963, Scribner's was reporting sales of 62,000) his royalty rate was to be scheduled at 17.5 percent. On January 24, 1963, Mitchell had to write and explain that the 17.5 percent rate applied to the *next book*, not *Thin Red Line*. By May 14, 1963, Jones had a royalty credit of $73,414.68. But his arrangement, for tax purposes, was to be paid through an account at Chase Manhattan in payments not to exceed $20,000 each August and February. With his considerable expenses in Paris, it was frustrating to try to live under the terms of the contract he had himself asked for. He could and did borrow against it and so was usually in debt, *behind* his actual earnings. The solution seemed to be the method of taking very large advances. Friends of his, including Irwin Shaw, had arranged their affairs this way, and it appeared to work.

In May of 1963, Jones wrote Mitchell that literary agent Scott Meredith had proposed a deal whereby Jones would receive an advance of $300,000, representing $150,000 each on two novels. He wondered what he should do about it.[22] Back came a letter from Mitchell, cautioning against dealing with Meredith, explaining that Scribner's could not match that offer because Scribner's had a policy against any "multi-book contract." But Mitchell proposed to offer $150,000 on the next book, to be arranged without agent or any agent's commission.[23] Jones got back to Mitchell, asking for a minimum of $150,000 each on the next two novels and that to be paid no matter what the royalties were on either book.[24] On June 14 Mitchell sent Jones a contract, fulfilling his requirements. (All of this was speedy business, conducted across the Atlantic.) On June 19, Jones returned the signed contract. For the next year he would be working on the "Underwater Novel," which would become *Go to the Widow-Maker*.

Next there was some bickering between Jones and Scribner's over an invitation Jones had received to attend the New York World's Fair for some kind of literary celebration. Scribner's refused to pay for his trip to New York. Communication was a little difficult at that moment (late February, early March 1964) because Jones was away and had a new secretary, Karen Weissberger, through whom Mitchell had to write to him. And in early March Jones suffered a serious leg injury while skiing at Klosters, Switzerland. He was operated on and recuperating at the hospital in Chur, a nearby town. Mitchell heard from Gloria, who gave him details of the accident and the operation and then, turning to the matter of the World's Fair, asked, "Why do you insist on antagonizing Jim since all the other publishers are footing the bill for their writers to come to this thing?"[25]

All that was smoothed over. Everybody got back to work. Another problem arose in May. Jones wanted to gather in the manuscripts of some of his earlier work. He had given Lowney Handy the manuscript of *Eternity* after the book was published. He hoped to get it back to give it to his daughter Kaylie. Nobody at Scribner's seemed to know what had happened to the original manuscripts of *Pistol* and *The Thin Red Line*. On June 15, 1964, Jones reported to Mitchell that he was suffering from a slipped disk. On June 29, Mitchell sent Jones the news that Lowney Handy had died in Florida during the past week. In August, Jones was vacationing in Trouville in Normandy, and, on September 14 he reported that he had scratched an eye with a grain of sand there.

On October 17, he wrote to Mitchell, "I am deeply involved with the 'Americans Abroad for Johnson' Campaign, and the main thing I have learned from it is that if this is democracy, dictators can't be so bad."[26]

On October 26 Jones heard from the law firm of Massey, Anderson & Gibson of Paris, Illinois, representing the estate of Lowney Handy, that no provision had been made by the late Mrs. Handy for the return of the manuscript of *Eternity* to Jones. Therefore, as her property, it was part of the estate and would go to her relatives. Pressure of business was mounting. In a letter of October 29 to his business manager in Chicago, Jones mentioned that several possible movie deals had fallen through. Early in November Jones reported to Mitchell that he had completed 150 pages of the new novel.[27]

In the meantime, thanks apparently to advice from Irwin Shaw and a number of other intermediaries, Jones had a large deal in the works. Ben

With Gloria at Deux Magots, Paris, 1960

With his buddy Irwin Shaw, early 1960s

Benjamin and Phyllis Jackson of the Ashley Famous Artists agency had arranged for two publishing companies, Dell and Pocket Books, to make separate contractual offers to Jones. Each was a complex, stepped contract with various escalator clauses, offering bonuses and increases according to the size of sales. Essentially, Dell offered an advance of $350,000 for the first book and $150,000 each on the second and third, plus all the complexity of "steps." His royalty was to be 17 percent in hardcover and 10 percent in paperback. Pocket Books came up with something similar—$300,000 for the first book, $200,000 for the second, and $150,000 for the third.

On November 19, 1964, Jones wrote Mitchell informing him that "in the last few days" he had received "a stupendous offer." He said that he could not avoid looking into it, and "if it checks out . . . accepting it." He said that he "never had any complaint, or not any very serious ones, about the way I have been treated at Scribner's." But this new arrangement would offer him financial security. "This is probably the hardest letter I've ever had to write. I think of you and Harry, and Cathie, and Wallace, and old Whitney and all the lunches and the hours hanging around the fifth floor and I don't really know if I can do it."[28]

A former editor remembers the shock and surprise at Scribner's the day that letter came in. "You know, though," he adds, "I think Charlie Scribner was glad. I really do. He was tired of Jones and his coarse and vulgar language and goosing the secretaries and all that. Charlie used to close his office door when he heard Jones coming."[29]

Glad or not (and Burroughs Mitchell, who, by then, was more dear friend than editor and was Jones's literary executor as well, must have been very sad), Scribner's was prompt. On November 23, 1964, Mitchell wrote him that there would be no counterproposal from Scribner's. Jones was free to accept another contract.

On December 21, 1964, came the contract from Dell, whose offer Jones had accepted. It called for hardcover publication by Delacorte and paperback publication by Dell. The first novel was to be delivered on or before January 1, 1968, the second by January 1, 1972, the third on January 1, 1976. The full potential of the contract was large, more than a million dollars. But, for the time being, until that first book was in, it meant payments, semiannually, of $35,000 a year for the next four years.

It was financial security for a time, provided he kept working and had a little luck.

For their interview, Jones took Arthur Goodfriend to see places in Paris which had taught him something. One of these was the Hôtel de Rouen where Sainte-Beuve had once lived. "I come here often," Jones said, "to reflect on the fact that Balzac actually bit himself in fury because he couldn't get a good review from Sainte-Beuve. Without this place to calm me down after reading reviews of *Widow-Maker*, I'd have chewed myself to death."[30]

In early 1965 Don Fine of Delacorte began to work with Jones as his editor. For openers he sent Jones a twenty-two-page, single-spaced editorial critique of the manuscript of the new novel. Jones seems to have been annoyed and distressed. Among his own notes concerning the manuscript Jones wrote: "I can no longer fully trust Fine's judgment because he looks at this novel not directly for what it attempts but thru a mirror first, mirror being his preconception of what a novel *ought* to be."[31] Jones missed Mitchell from the outset, and there appears to have been a limited sympathy between Jones and Fine. Later Jones's editor was Ross Claiborne, but an obituary statement by Claiborne implies a kind of friction that was simply not there with Mitchell. "He was a brilliant craftsman who had revised draft after draft of his work before he let us see it," Claiborne is quoted as saying. "When it finally got to us, it was very hard for him to allow changes."[32]

Go to the Widow-Maker (1967) was the first book delivered under the new Dell/Delacorte contract. It was a novel with all the ingredients of a blockbuster. Ample in scope, straightforward in sequence and telling, it was "a good read." There was an exotic setting—Jamaica and the Bahamas. It offered a cast of seemingly glamorous characters, a behind-the-scenes look at attractive, successful, glittery people. And it had an intriguing touch of roman à clef. The protagonist, Ron Grant, a leading young Broadway playwright, was not radically unlike the known public image of Jones himself; Lucia Angelina Elena (Lucky) Videndi, first Ron's lover, then his wife, shared some history and characteristics with Gloria Mosolino Jones; Hunt and Carol Abernathy showed some common elements of the lives and characters of Harry and Lowney Handy; Carol Abernathy's Hunt Hills Little Theatre Group closely resembled Lowney's Handy Writers' Colony. And many of the other characters, identified as celebrities of one kind and another, were evidently based upon real figures. There was a steady, mounting, suspenseful line of action dealing with the excitement and dangers of skin diving. Finally, there was plenty of sex, in a variety of forms, real and fantasized, practiced by the lively cast. All these things, however, are simply given and expected elements of the popular (or public) novel. Clearly Jones wanted to succeed in those terms, and he met the requirements of the game well enough so that the novel overall has achieved considerable commercial success, especially in paperback, where it has been kept in print by Dell, going through sixteen reprintings and then a new printing, as well, by April 1979.

But Jones was always a truth seeker and a truth teller as well as a solid professional craftsman. True to himself, he wanted to make something much more than merely one more example of the genre. In the dedication to his daughter Kaylie, Jones announces it as a "love story," and so it is, demonstrating dramatically how, gradually and painfully, two young people, Ron and Lucky, can overcome the pressures of society and the inward pressures of their complex and separate personal psychological histories to find and keep each other. To do this honestly in his own terms and effectively in terms of narrative, Jones had to present them in the same harsh light as he did his other characters. His characters are, one and all, mixed, ambivalent, frequently confused, often wrongheaded, and very seldom completely sympathetic. To deal directly with the sex lives of these characters, he was required, as he had been in *Some Came Running* (though this time he had the distinct advantage of a much more lively, entertaining story line), to move forward by fits and starts, through a series of gradual, cumulative revelations—a kind of psychological striptease. Jones also chose to treat something else, which was inherent in the material but which could have been cleverly ignored—the subject of male courage and its relationship to sexuality. If in his war novels, especially in *The Thin Red Line*, Jones had seriously questioned some of Hemingway's well-known, almost mythical (and popular) notions, here Jones challenged the old master openly (and satirically), since most of these characters were literate enough to have read Hemingway and to have been influenced by his work. Indeed, much in *Widow-Maker* can be seen as a critique of the terms of Hemingway's fictional world.

Jones was completely serious about the accuracy and authenticity of the skin-diving and sailing scenes in the novel. Among the papers at the Beinecke Library, together with many drafts of the novel, are various charts and graphs, drawings and records of depths of dives and time required, of tides and prevailing winds and currents. Jones had maps to refresh his memory of Jamaica. And Gloria Jones reports that Jones spent hours in the water working out the precise details of the dives in the novel. Facts were important in his fiction, and authenticity was more than a decorative trope. Jones used a shifting and universal point of view for the story, a choice which was demanded by the need to explore the differences between appearance and reality in his characters, particularly in terms of sexuality. And, as in *Some Came Running*, he told the whole story in "colloquial forms," that loose, easygoing, altogether American contemporary idiom (with all its flaws as well as its virtues) which he was developing, pushing closer to the edge of first-person, spoken telling. Ideally, this kind of language should appropriately fit each of the characters and yet be so direct and simple as to seem transparent. But even at its best the method runs two great risks: first, the problem of authorial identification, the need on the part of some readers and many reviewers to attribute to the author the thoughts and feelings of various characters; secondly, the serious possibility that the reader may miss some or much of what is intended to be funny, though it may be deadly serious to the characters. This latter is particularly troublesome in intimate matters, for example in the sexual practices of the characters, which, no matter how patently grotesque or absurd, are more painful than comic to many readers.

One thing more should be added concerning Jones's use of autobiographical material. It is clear that Jones habitually used characteristics of himself and people he knew well, together with events from his own life and theirs, as models, starting points for his fiction. The more we know about him, the more obvious this becomes. But Jones was not really an autobiographical novelist. In *Go to the Widow-Maker* those facts about himself which were public knowledge were deliberately used for public purposes, but those things which were, in fact, private were used for private reasons. Unless the author calls attention to the connections between and relationships to his "real" life and his fictions, it is usually unwise, a waste of time at the least, to look for signs of and clues to their secret presence.

Go to the Widow-Maker was greeted with mixed reviews. And those which were negative managed to rise to a high tone of derision. Peter Sourian, writing for *Commonweal*, led off his review with a personal note. "Having undertaken to review a book before reading it, on the strength of its having been written by a man who has written books you value, and finding you have a bad book on your hands, you ask yourself whether or not to beg off from the task."[33] *Library Journal*, usually strong for Jones, called it "repetitious" and "tedious," yet added that "Jones's writing is as virile as ever, and many of his minor characters leap instantly to life."[34] But that was purely kind and generous compared to the more typical approach to the novel, spelled out by Josh Greenfeld in the *New York Times Book Review*. Greenfeld called it "an utter embarrassment, possessing only the kinship of genus and bulk to its antecedents," adding that there was "almost nothing to recommend it." He described Jones as going "on and on, relentlessly, like an electrically operated toy animal." His conclusion was "It will probably bear the dubious distinction of being the worst book by a good writer to be published this year."[35]

What turned out to be one of the most thorough review-essays done on Jones and his work up to that point was the *Atlantic* review of *Widow-Maker* by Wilfrid Sheed. Superficially it was a firmly negative and determinedly witty hatchet job on the new novel, characteristics which would have rendered Sheed's remarks no more than typical:

> Technically, there is little danger of Jones's ever becoming any good. His prose, struggle manfully with it as he may, remains a sneer-and-grin, pulp-fiction prose. His philosophical disquisitions sound like second-drawer reform-school bull sessions. His dialogue is wooden and undifferentiated, to the point where you can scarcely tell the girls from the boys. And to make assurance doubly sure, he seems to have passed beyond the reach of normal editorial protection against himself.[36]

But then, even after allowing that this novel "is almost worthless," Sheed begins to discuss Jones's special gifts. He duly notes his "vulnerability to experience," but adds that there are all too many writers with that gift. What he singles out as Jones's special power as a writer "is that rarest of blessings or curses, a private obsession that picks up echoes everywhere, an obsession of public value." He calls this obsession "a quasi-prophetic gift" which made possible the best of his work, which Sheed identifies as *Eternity* and *Thin Red Line*. Then Sheed deals with *Widow-Maker* and its cousin, *Some Came Running*, as parts of the same larger story, the same world view. It is Sheed's argument that these works, and specifically

Widow-Maker, are flawed and "meaningless outside the larger context." All the stories are to be not so much measured by as understood in terms of the truths of *Eternity* and *Thin Red Line*, and in those terms they make a desperate, coherent sense. But Sheed sees Jones as out of touch with the times, "a Pierce-Arrow among contemporary novelists."

> The danger right now is that he finds himself with less to say to fewer people. His vagrant romanticism and his bulging wallet make him a rather special case anyway, but not without interest: what hurts is that his roots in World War II are beginning to look quaint. His abstention from regular civil life; from child rearing and job promotions on the one hand or relevant opposition to these on the other, has kept him stuck in the past, and this cuts him off finally even from his own generation.[37]

What Sheed could not possibly have realized at the time was how close he was to describing Jones's own awareness of his situation and, more important, his general plan for the future. For in the years ahead, from among many potential subjects (Jones never had any paucity of subjects for novels in mind), he would essentially be doing two separate yet related things: (1) reclaiming and restoring his past with *Ice-Cream Headache*, *WWII*, and above all *Whistle*, and (2) dealing with the rapidly changing and shifting scene of the 1960s in *The Merry Month of May* (mainly concerned with the Paris student rebellion of 1968) and in *A Touch of Danger*, which placed his middle-aged detective, Lobo Davis, on a Greek island amid the international youth and (well-to-do) hippie scene. *Viet Journal* would do a little of both, for the narrative body would be contemporary reportage, but in the "Epilogue: Hawaiian Recall" Jones would bring *now* and *then* together in harmony.

The most interesting fact about Sheed's piece is that Jones must have read it, and with some care; later, when he returned to America he and Sheed became friends. Jones was not able to be friendly with people he deemed to be completely wrong or dishonest. It says something for Jones's maturity and sanity that, at a crucial time in his life and career, he was able to read beyond obvious offense to comprehend the deeper argument and that he could judge it to be honestly meant and even of value.

He would need that maturity when *The Merry Month of May* came along. *Ice-Cream Headache* (1968) received limited coverage, as is often the case with books of stories, but the reviews were favorable. But *Merry Month of May* brought out the sharks.

The Merry Month of May (1971) is told in the first person by one Jonathan James Hartley III, a surprising narrator for Jones to choose. Hartley is editor of a literary magazine, *The Two Islands Review*, and describes himself as "a failed poet, a failed novelist" and "a drop-out of a husband. . . ." He is a close friend of the Gallaghers from Boston—Harry, a successful screenwriter, Louisa, his wife, their college-age son, Hill, who is a student at the Sorbonne, and the young daughter, McKenna, who is Hartley's godchild—who live in an apartment much like that of the Joneses and maintain a somewhat similar life-style, allowing, among other things, for the introduction of a large number of American and European characters. Hartley and the Gallaghers, like Jones, live on the Île St.-Louis. The story is told from the vantage point of mid-June 1968, immediately following the collapse of the student uprising, or "revolution," which had preoccupied Paris throughout the month of May. It offers a history of that uprising, filtered through Hartley's point of view, which turns out to be a fairly close approximation of the author's even-handed approach to public events—that there was some virtue and a lot of foolishness on both sides. The novel details the breakup of the Gallaghers' lives during that tense, stressful period (son Hill is deeply involved with the students). The Gallaghers' marital difficulties are exacerbated by the uprising, but their immediate personal disasters are precipitated by the catalytic effect of an attractive, bisexual, black young woman—Samantha-Marie Everton. Their story ends with Harry in Tel Aviv in pursuit of the sensual Samantha, with Louisa as a failed suicide, severely brain-damaged, in Paris, and with Hartley (not entirely guiltless himself) left to pick up all the pieces. Shorter by half than any of Jones's other major novels and (necessarily) told in a more polished style, *The Merry Month of May* is also the novel in which Jones makes the most extensive and functional use of *place*. Paris, surviving all tragedies, public and domestic, is brilliantly, lovingly evoked, becoming, in essence, a central character in the story. The picture of the student revolt may be debatable; certainly it differs from most advocacy accounts, both in fiction and nonfiction. And the continuing scrutiny by Jones of American sexual maladjustment may seem, as it did to any number of negative critics, to be psychologically primitive. But the realization of Paris as an exciting, *living* force in the novel is extraordinary and shows another dimension of Jones's sensibility.

Some of the reviews were favorable. Robert H. Donahugh (again) gave it a fine send-off in *Library Journal*: "No review can indicate the excitement and passion of this, Jones' best novel since *From Here to Eternity*."[38] It was described by Raymond A. Sokolov in the *New York Times Book Review* as "the best account in English of the May Days—and [he] also put Paris on paper as knowingly as any Anglo-Saxon has ever done."[39] No mild claim. But a great many other reviewers were less than kind. For some reason (perhaps political?) the literary quarterlies, which had usually ignored Jones's work, came forward to review this one. In the *Hudson Review* William H. Pritchard decided on the basis of the book, "that Jones may be the victim of creeping self-satisfaction."[40] Kenneth John Atchity had stronger words in the *Mediterranean Review*: "I have often wished that the God of Books would grant to each reviewer, once in a lifetime, the right to have any writer taken out of circulation and quietly strangled—without any question, any explanation. Jones would be my choice. If justice itself is more than a word, then such an all-encompassing misuse of words as Jones is guilty of will not go without retribution."[41] But one didn't have to hunt among the greater and lesser literary magazines. *Newsweek* (in the person of Geoffrey Wolff) which had usually been somewhat sympathetic, at least more often than *Time*, lowered the boom on Jones and *Merry Month*: "Jones writes so badly that his offenses constitute as great a crime against nature as against literature. A book written this badly shouldn't be called a book."[42]

As Sheed's treatment of *Widow-Maker* had been the principal essay-review, so the major piece on *Merry Month of May* was to come from another prominent literary critic, John W. Aldridge, in the *Saturday Review*. Aldridge had known Jones in the early 1950s, "the young days," when Aldridge and Bourjaily were coediting *Discovery* and were companions of Mailer, Styron, and Jones. They had been together at a literary conference in France, at Blérancourt in the spring of 1959. And Aldridge had dealt generally with the whole group of post–World War II writers in a *New York Times Book Review* piece (July 29, 1962). There Aldridge had concerned himself with "the failure of these writers to develop artistically or to continue their novelistic careers." The *Saturday Review* piece was a devastating dismissal of Jones and the kind of novel he was devoting his

tion of this Revolution! Including the one at Harry
Gallagher's!"

        After he left, I wondered if his very last remark
was not still a further allusion to these papers, to his
awareness of their existence, and that he was giving me
permission--no, was <u>asking</u> me, please to include him in
anything I wrote about the Gallaghers. History he wanted.
Well, I would certain^{LY} have to include him. He certainly
did play a role. A key role. But somehow it depressed
me. It depressed me even more than I had known that
seeing him would do, and I went myself to my window. I
leaned on the protective wrought-iron railing, looking
out at the sadness of the flowing river. As Weintraub
had done. IT WAS ALWAYS THERE, THAT SADNESS OF THE RIVER, OF THE FLOWING OF
THE RIVER.
BUT I'VE NEVER
BEEN ABLE TO
ISOLATE WHY.
IT WAS
IT ALWAYS SEEMED
SO SAD.

BUT

*[WORK IN]
'THAT WAS ONE
THING I COULD
COUNT ON.*

LC /   Night ~~had~~ had fallen since he had arrived. And the
Paris streetlights had come on along the quai. Across
the river, lights were coming on in the Left Bank apartments.
And in the <u>Quartier</u> itself there were no more thuds of
gas grenades igniting, no more fires flickering from
barracades to light up the rising clouds of smoke and
tear gas, no more flashes and the cracking reports of the
percussion grenades. Something indeed had truly ended.

        By leaning out I could look up the quai to the /LC

Manuscript page from The Merry
Month of May (Humanities Research
Center, University of Texas at
Austin)

*Trees chopped down to serve as
barricades during riots, Paris,
May 1968* (photo by Jones)

life to writing. Aldridge described him as possessing "a thoroughly commonplace mind seemingly arrested forever at the level of its adolescent ideas about experience and literature." "Long years of residence in Paris," Aldridge wrote, "seem to have taught him very little except the right places to go eat lunch." As for his "approach to fiction," it is defined as "antiquated and provincial, not because it is no longer in fashion, but because it can no longer be depended upon to yield a valid or original impression of reality."[43]

In truth, Jones had learned, was learning many things in Paris. One of them concerned the critics and their relationship with the artist. Shortly after that conference at Blérancourt he wrote to critic-scholar Robert W. Stallman who had also been there. "A certain amount of self-conscious knowledge can only help a novelist who has any brains at all," Jones wrote. "I learned that at Blérancourt. Too much of the same thing could be killing; I learned that at lunch."[44]

Because he had, at that time, still been spared extensive academic experience, Jones missed arriving at a truth which might have eased some pains—that critics are primarily concerned with (and competitive with) *other critics*: that novels and novelists, likewise poems and poets, plays and playwrights, are only of importance as occasions for the creation of *criticism*; that therefore there is no real harm intended no matter how much harm may be done; that sooner or later, because that is how reputation and success are arrived at in the field, one critic will cancel out another by wrestling a different interpretation from precisely the same material; that you can bet that any strong position will, as if by Newtonian physics, evoke a counterattack of equal force. If the late 1960s were a low point for Jones among many of the literati, the early 1970s showed how things could turn. For example another prominent critic of recent writing, Ihab Hassan, in *Contemporary American Literature 1945–1972: An Introduction* (1973), went out of his way to chide his peers and to make a case for Jones: "Jones is accused of uncouth writing, sensationalism, and naivete; but though he sometimes gives evidence of these faults, he possesses gifts greater than subtlety: a capacity to respond to life in narrative terms, enduring honesty in statement, a covert uncanny sensitivity."[45]

But Jones had very little time or energy to spend studying the ups and downs of his critical reputation except insofar as it might have a direct practical impact on book sales and deals. He kept his clippings and kept on working. To write *Whistle* and to finish the war trilogy was his chief concern, even though he had to put it aside to finish other things. He also had to put aside, forever as it happened, another long-standing project: the jazz novel, based on the figure of Django Reinhardt, to be set in Paris at the end of World War II and called "No Peace I Find."

At the time Arthur Goodfriend was writing his in-depth piece about Jones for *Saturday Review*, Jones was finishing up *The Merry Month of May*. And that is the Jones who emerges in the article, an American who knows Paris well and loves it deeply. There are the almost obligatory references to the Sunday night suppers and the kind of company, the Gothic pulpit, and the spiral staircase. And he describes the studio upstairs where Jones had written, by that time, *The Thin Red Line, The Ice-Cream Headache,* and *Go to the Widow-Maker*. But this article takes Jones out into Paris; to L'Escole, a bar on the corner of Rue des Deux Ponts, where Jones plays pinball, to Brasserie de l'Île St.-Louis at 55, Quai de Bourbon, a favorite eating place for Jones and Gloria. "Plain as a wooden Alsatian shoe," Goodfriend writes, "the Brasserie lays down on paper-covered boards the tastiest tripe, cassoulets, and choucroutes garnies in Paris, and its Murzig beer, Jones swore, is France's best."[46] Talk of food and drink leads to an account of Chez René, the Left Bank restaurant at 14, Boulevard Saint-Germain. Both of these quite different places figure prominently in *The Merry Month of May*. There were other places he pointed out to Goodfriend, places which also had a part in the world of *The Merry Month of May*; for example, Confucius, a Vietnamese restaurant at 81, Rue St.-Louis-en-l'Île, and Le Nuage at 5, Bernard PaLissy, just off Saint-Germain-des-Prés, with its famous drink, the Nuage Special, an adroit mixture of vodka, crème de cacao and a dash of grenadine.

Sooner or later, as it was bound to, the subject of Hemingway comes up. In one sense, perhaps not even consciously, Jones's escape to Europe in 1958 had been an attempt to touch base with the past. Just as he had gone first to the desk of Maxwell Perkins, now he had come to Paris, rich with the tradition of the American literary expatriates. In 1963 he had followed in the master's footsteps, gone down with a crowd of friends to Pamplona in Spain for eight days for the running of the bulls, and had written it up for *Esquire*. It had not been an altogether satisfactory experience, and in part he blamed Hemingway for that.[47] Now, however, he had Paris as a test for Hemingway's integrity. And he concluded that Hemingway did not measure up, at least by the standards Jones lived for and by. Jones said this to Goodfriend:

> I bought a copy of *A Moveable Feast* and spent three days trying to trace the places he described. . . . Hemingway's Paris doesn't exist. The book really isn't about Paris. It's about Hemingway. It shocked and horrified me, the egomania of the man. One has to be an egomaniac to be a writer, but you have to hide it. Hemingway was more concerned with being an international celebrity than in writing great books. He worked harder on his image than on his integrity.[48]

His own attitude, openly expressed to Goodfriend in what, after all, was basically a public relations situation, was sane and mature.

Aside from his problems as writer, Jones found himself under more mundane pressures in Paris than he had known in Marshall during the 1950s. Establishing residency and then maintaining it in Paris had proved to be enormously complex, a bureaucratic nightmare. Handling finances, in more than one currency and under several forms of regulation, required the services of more lawyers and accountants and bankers—in London, in Paris, in Zurich. Probably one of the simplest problems he had to face was what to do with his Yugoslavian royalties, which could not be removed from that country but only spent there. The result of that bureaucratic rigidity was a wonderful vacation, with friends, in Dubrovnik, where he rented a yacht and enjoyed excellent skin-diving off the Dalmatian coast. It would have been a perfect time except that Kaylie Jones, barely a year old, became desperately ill with diphtheria and almost died. This disease, which has all but vanished from the American scene, is still to be found, occasionally, in Europe where children are not routinely inoculated against it.

Jones's day-to-day stress level was high: the pressure of business affairs; pressure (however pleasant) from the constant stream of friends and acquaintances and friends of friends; the pressure of the baffling times, the uproarious 1960s seen from overseas; the pressure of still having to pay his dues, helping beginning writers, offering aid and comfort to his often beleaguered peers; pressures of health, for since the summer of 1959 at Portofino, Italy, where he had suffered an attack involving his heart and circulation, he had had to be very careful of himself (to reassure Mitchell he wrote, September 14, 1959, that "I just have to cut down on the boozing, smoking, overeating"). All these things worked on him. And, for all the money he had earned and was scheduled to earn, the cash flow was never quite enough to keep up with mounting expenses, with the style of living he had adopted and the kinds of people, some of them among the true rich, he often associated with. Still, it was, year by year, *almost* enough for everything, close enough so that, until the end, it would have seemed foolish ingratitude toward lady luck to cut back too much.

And just when things looked bleak or hopeless, something would happen. According to Gloria Jones, they once went down to Deauville and actually *gambled* their way back to solvency—he at the card table, she at roulette. In 1972, when things were not going well and the only new property Jones had on hand was "A Touch of Sun"—the "novelization" of a failed screen treatment, something which did not fit into the elaborate contractual context and scheme of Dell/Delacorte and which Dell had chosen to ignore—just then, out of the fairy-tale blue, came a traveling Doubleday editor, Lee Barker. He offered Jones an advance of close to $200,000 for it, with the idea that there would be a future Lobo Davis suspense series from Jones.

A Touch of Danger is a suspense story, taut and fast-moving, in the classic hard-boiled manner, featuring a tough, aging, cynical American private eye—Lobo Davis. Davis, about Jones's age and sharing some personal history with the author, tells the story in the first person. The tale is set in Greece and specifically on the fictional island of Tsatsos, much like Spétsai where the Joneses had vacationed. The ingredients, as accurately described on the back cover of the Popular Library paperback edition, include "a beautiful, blackmailed Countess, ruthless tycoons, violent hippies, dope smuggling, twisted loves—and a brutal taste of murder." It also allows for some excellent set pieces on boat handling and skin diving and some elegant evocation of place. Lobo has a somewhat jaundiced view of the counterculture of dopers and hippies, but all his prejudices are not confirmed, and he finds he is not too old to learn a thing or two. Probably the most interesting fact about *A Touch of Danger* is the pure skill of it. As entertainment, as a genre piece, it holds up with the best of them and proves (if it needed proving) that Jones had the craft and the capacity to write economically and well within the strict limits of the thriller, that he was a more versatile writer than at least some of the critics had imagined.

With Yugoslavian divers on a summer trip to Dalmatian coast, 1960s

In his study at "Il Castelleto," Portofino, Italy, 1959 (The Photo Shop, Portofino, Italy)

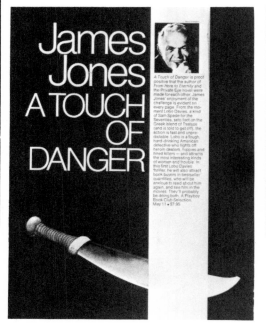

James Jones
A TOUCH
OF
DANGER

A Touch of Danger is proof positive that the author of From Here to Eternity and The Pistol have never been made for each other. James Jones' enjoyment of the challenge is evident on every page. From the moment Lobo Davies, a kind of Sam Spade for the Seventies, sets foot on the Greek island of Tsatsos (and is told to get off), the action is fast and unpredictable. Lobo is a tough, hard-drinking American detective who fights off heroin dealers, hippies and hired killers — and attracts the most interesting kinds of women and trouble. In this first Lobo Davies thriller, he will also attract book buyers in bestseller quantities, who will be anxious to read about him again, and see him in the movies. They'll probably be doing both. A Playboy Book Club Selection. May 11 • $7.95

Cartoon celebrating Gloria's luck and skill at cards, Paris, 1970

LEFT: Publishers Weekly *cover ad, March 1973*

With Gloria and Kaylie about to board the La France, *1962*

With his family rowing on the Marne, mid-1960s

As the "skipper" sailing Greek isles, early 1970s

Gloria Jones reports that though the story is mostly imaginary, many details have a factual basis. And Matthew J. Bruccoli writes: "Jones told me that the central gimmick actually happened. He was vacationing in Greece when a body was found, and local cops decided that it was 'a hairless ape'—not a man—in order to avoid upsetting tourist business."[49]

Barker, the editor, would die before *A Touch of Danger* was published, and Jones would be dead before he could do a second suspense novel, but at that moment it was a blessing. Pure luck.

"We had so much fun in those days," Gloria Jones remembers. And they certainly did. From the beginning their lives were not confined to Paris. There were trips to Spain and Italy and Germany and vacations in delightful places. To Jamaica (Lilliput Beach House, Montego Bay) and the West Indies (West Indian Club, Georgetown, Grand Cayman) to sun and swim and skin-dive, escaping the dead of winter. To small, beautiful Klosters in Canton Grisons, with its ancient monastery of St. Jakob, its celebrated church with clock tower, all set high in the Prättigau Valley and surrounded by mountains, for skiing and winter sports. To lush Spétsai, among Greece's Saronic Gulf Islands and splendidly located at the mouth of the Gulf of Argolis (this island was made famous more recently by John Fowles in *The Magus*). To ancient walled, proudly independent Dubrovnik. To Portofino on Italy's beautiful Riviera di Levante. There is—was, in those days still—a common pattern to all of these places. They were small, choice, unspoiled by too much tourism, places of permanent houses and residents rather than transients. Often the residents included celebrities. In Portofino, for example, their neighbors and friends were Rex Harrison and Kay Kendall. And all of these places were beautiful. The views of harbor and sea, from Spétsai or from the high house they rented in Portofino, are matchless.

At Klosters, while skiing in March 1964, Jones had a serious fall, which required surgery for ankle and knee. He had hurt his legs in a traffic accident earlier in Paris (and, according to Gloria, had been thoroughly beaten up by the French police), but after this accident, his skiing days were over. As in other things, he turned this wound into words, writing up the experience in "Letter Home" for *Esquire* (December 1964), the moment of hospital treatment taking him all the way back to the war: "When I came out, there was the same old confusion of bright lights flashing, faces wheeling, people banging, people yelling. God, it was all so familiar!"[50]

The greatest pleasure, however, for Jones and Gloria was their family, daughter Kaylie and son Jamie. Gloria had suffered a number of miscarriages, the first in London's Hotel Stafford in 1958, and more than one tubal pregnancy. It took great care for Kaylie to be brought into the world. And when Gloria could not have more children of her own, they adopted a young child they already knew and loved from Jamaica. Amid everything else, it was ultimately his family that came first with Jones.

The last place that Jones took Arthur Goodfriend, for the sake of Goodfriend's article, was to look at a memorial in honor of the Martyrs of the Deportation, some 200,000 Jews and Gypsies and other "undesirables" sent to their deaths during the Nazi occupation. Jones evidently wanted Goodfriend to understand what he made of it, what knowledge of the meaning of evil in the world he had arrived at through the hard school of experience. It must have been especially important to Jones at that time, for with *The Merry Month of May* in the works and *A Touch of Danger* close behind it, and both of these dealing in part with the youth rebellion of the 1960s as well as the vision of the world which inspired contemporary youth, he had to measure his own earned wisdom against theirs.

The spirit of the 1960s is quite accurately represented by writer and film critic Richard Grenier, in an article for the *New York Times*, March 6, 1983. Describing the attitude (his own) of the youth of the time, Grenier writes:

> Now during the 60's and continuing through the 70's, if in somewhat sanitized form, there came upon the land a new set of beliefs, which, however clumsy or ill-expressed, had a distinctly utopian flavor, and often appeared as an ill-thought-out and half-baked anarchism. Central to anarchist thought, however, is the conviction that man is naturally good and that he is corrupted only by such artificial institutions as the state. Hence a whole generation of the affluent American young . . . believed that evil could be easily located in soldiers, policemen, William Calley and Richard Nixon.[51]

(One of the letters Jones wrote to Mitchell from Paris was a letter trying to help a writer named Richard Grenier get published.)[52] In that same issue of *The New York Times*, another writer out of the 1960s, playwright Ronald Ribman, makes a somewhat similar argument: "I have a feeling that

With General Weyland, 1973

OPPOSITE: *Manuscript page from* Viet Journal (Humanities Research Center, University of Texas at Austin)

In Saigon during research for Viet Journal, *1973*

1/VIET JOURNAL

JONES

(A)

THE CALL [U3]

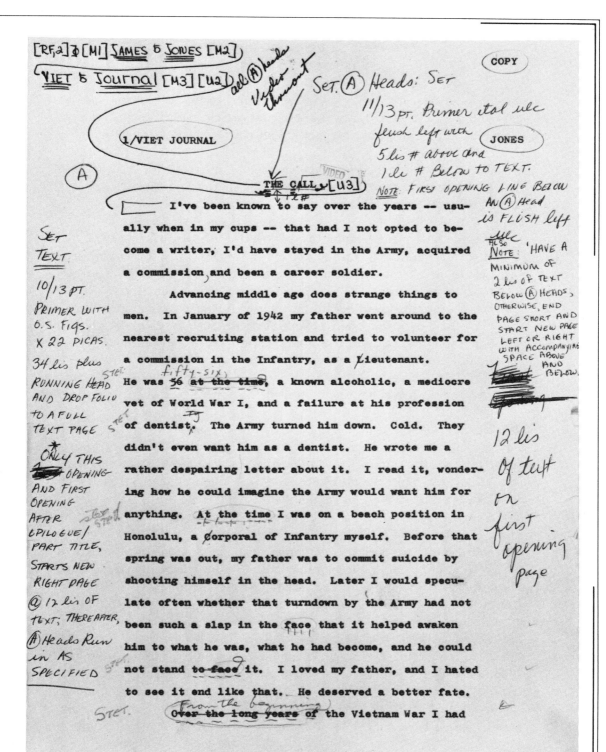

I've been known to say over the years -- usually when in my cups -- that had I not opted to become a writer, I'd have stayed in the Army, acquired
a commission, and been a career soldier.

Advancing middle age does strange things to
men. In January of 1942 my father went around to the
nearest recruiting station and tried to volunteer for
a commission in the Infantry, as a Lieutenant.
He was 56 *fifty-six* at the time, a known alcoholic, a mediocre
vet of World War I, and a failure at his profession
of dentist. The Army turned him down. Cold. They
didn't even want him as a dentist. He wrote me a
rather despairing letter about it. I read it, wondering how he could imagine the Army would want him for
anything. At the time I was on a beach position in
Honolulu, a Corporal of Infantry myself. Before that
spring was out, my father was to commit suicide by
shooting himself in the head. Later I would speculate often whether that turndown by the Army had not
been such a slap in the face that it helped awaken
him to what he was, what he had become, and he could
not stand to face it. I loved my father, and I hated
to see it end like that. He deserved a better fate.
STET From the beginning Over the long years of the Vietnam War I had

most of the neurotic behavior we see is the result of external pressure deforming a character. It's when love and caring are withheld, when people's basic needs are not only not satisfied but trampled on that you get deformity."[53]

Jones, though he had long ago claimed an affinity with the anarchists, had a different view of the source of evil in the world. Looking at the memorial to the Martyrs he remarked:

> It's the best place I know to consider the history of violence and its effect on the human race. I don't mean only war, but the violence of nature, of plagues, of famine, of storms and earthquakes, of amoeba feeding on each other. The human race isn't violent by choice. The human race is violent because it lives on a planet created and based on violence. There's no one to blame for war, for genocide, for chopping down innocent trees to build barricades—not Napoleon, not Hitler, or Cohn-Bendit. We must blame ourselves. We must learn to control the earthly violence within each of us. We must move out of primitive violence toward something better of the spirit.[54]

During his last year in Paris, with *The Merry Month of May* and *A Touch of Danger* behind him, Jones went off to find real violence again, to report on the situation in Vietnam during the final days before the American withdrawal of forces on March 28, 1973. This was done on assignment for *The New York Times Magazine*. But, having come up with the idea, the *Times*, it turned out, lacked the clout or craft to get him where he wanted to go. Hanoi was out of the question. Even Jones's friend, Mary McCarthy, who had been there and was chummy with the North Vietnamese, could not fix it. And in South Vietnam he wanted to go where fighting was still taking place (in violation of the truce) and see for himself what no other American journalist could at that time. He was able to arrange this because of his personal friendship with General Frederick C. Weyand (the book is dedicated "To Fred and Arline Weyand . . .") who had once commanded the 25th, the Tropic Lightning Division, Jones's old outfit, in Vietnam in 1965. Jones had come to know Weyand in Paris after that, and now, in 1973, Weyand was a full general, second in command in Vietnam and commander of Military Assistance Command, Vietnam. Weyand made it possible, and Jones went to see for himself. He went to war and saw it and reported on it, what was happening at the headquarters, and in the hospitals, in the various staging areas and, more dangerously, what was going on at remote and isolated fire bases. He met the fighting men and spent long sessions talking freely with his own contemporaries in the military, who were now the middle-aged, high-ranking officers who were leading the war effort. The reporting is first-rate and even has some quality of hard news, since nobody else was able to cover some of the stories he did. But there was more to it. When he returned, he wrote of the experience in a cool, objective, matter-of-fact manner. He did not take sides in the passionate political arguments which, on both sides, allowed room for only heroes and villains, but he was fearless enough and honest enough to express admiration for courage and competency where he saw it, and he was almost unique in choosing not to ignore mention of the horrendous atrocities which had been committed by the Viet Cong and the North Vietnamese during the Tet Offensive of 1968 and afterward. To this reportage Jones added an overtly and deeply personal element. *Viet Journal* opens with a brief, moving recollection of his father and his father's suicide. It ends with a powerful, wonderfully vivid account of Jones's stopover in Hawaii on the way home from Vietnam, of his return to the places of his days as a young soldier, the places where the action of *From Here to Eternity* was played out.

By October he was writing Michael Mewshaw about it:

I am very pleased with the Vietnam book. . . . I think it is very readable. No chapter headings, no section headings, just this series of vignettes and small essays on such things as GARBAGE, TEETH, TOILETS, interlaced with pieces of action and description and character studies about the things and people I met. It is not very anti-American.[55]

The book was done, he was pleased with it, pleased to tell this younger novelist about it. But the real reason he was writing to Mewshaw was that Jones was looking for a way to come home.[56]

*I was in New York in July to do some TV
shows and interviews and while there had a
long discussion with my lawyer. He thinks
it would be beneficial for me to come back
to the States next year, probably as soon
as the school year ends here—which means
the end of May or middle of June.*

James Jones[1]

*I was always like a bird on a branch in Paris.
I was never part of it. And I found,
increasingly, that I just didn't understand
the French mind.*

James Jones[2]

PART FIVE
• • •
HOME TO WHISTLE

MIAMI

Why would a writer whose trademark had
always been toughness and independence,
a writer supposedly contemptuous of critics
and impatient with intellectuals, a writer
reputed to have been rich—why would such
a man teach?

Michael Mewshaw[3]

· · ·

B Y the fall of 1973 there were good reasons for Jones to think about
moving home to the United States. Lawyers advised it; the tax advantages
of foreign residency had diminished and so had the value of the dollar. It
was costing too much to continue to live in Paris. And there wasn't enough
money coming in these days and wouldn't be, either, until he could finish
Whistle. *A Touch of Danger* had not done as well as hoped, selling only
19,717 copies in hardcover. And even with good notices, the cover of *Publishers Weekly* for the first time since *Eternity*, major advertising, selection
by the Playboy Book Club, and sale of reprint rights to Popular Library, it
had not recovered its advance. *Viet Journal* was coming up, but it did not
look likely to be a strong commercial book. Then there was the matter of
the children's education. James and Gloria Jones wanted their children to
have the experience of high school in America. In a few years they would
be applying to college. Jones wanted to see that his children had every
chance to enjoy the best possible American college education (which he

had missed), and he wanted, if he could manage it, to leave them adequately provided for, at least well-off enough to have a fair chance of surviving in a bitterly competitive, inflationary world. Jones was concerned about his health. He was not feeling well. Perhaps some of it was homesickness. They were ready to come home.

There were problems about leaving, however. Most of Jones's assets, his largest single investment like that of most Americans, were in his home —the Paris apartment, that wonderful apartment into which they had poured so much care and attention and money. He wanted to hold out and hold on to the property, if he possibly could, until he could get the best price for it. That would take time and patience—another gamble. Perhaps his biggest one. Meantime, however, they would need some kind of immediate cash flow, a way to live at home until he could get his business affairs straightened out.

Jones thought that maybe a teaching job would fit the bill, a writer in residence position in one of the universities. Where didn't matter a whole lot, though he thought he would prefer somewhere out west, because he still had in mind to write a novel set in the West. Tentatively, innocently, for he knew of the contemporary relationship between writers and the academies only from second hand, he began to see what he could do.

Here we must turn to the young novelist Michael Mewshaw, Jones's friend who was teaching English at the time at the University of Texas. Mewshaw has written this up for *The Nation*, and the letters he exchanged with Jones about it are preserved at the Humanities Research Center. His first letter to Mewshaw concerning this matter was written September 14, 1973. Jones was hoping that Mewshaw could get something arranged at the University of Texas. He could not. For now Texas wasn't interested. Nor, Mewshaw discovered, scouting around a bit (for he felt a friendly obligation to help as much as he could), were most of the other major institutions that regularly hire visiting writers or have some program in creative writing. To his surprise he found that most places frankly felt Jones lacked the kind of "visibility" they were looking for.

Mewshaw carefully contacted major American institutions, directly or through friends; they had an opportunity to hire Jones and turned it down precisely on the grounds of "visibility" and doubts as to Jones's teaching ability. Still, Mewshaw assumed that Jones would have no real problem, for Jones's many friends in the literary world, including some of the most distinguished and "visible" writers in the country, would rally around and find a place for him. They did not—this time at least. It fell to Mewshaw, acting as a kind of agent, to handle it all for Jones, who was still in France and had no idea about how much money he could expect or what an institution would expect of him. He was willing to do what he had to, but wanted the best possible deal. It came down to a choice between the Iowa Writers Workshop, with which Jones had been dealing directly, and Florida International University, a new institution in Miami, were Harry Antrim, chairman of English and one of the original organizers of FIU, was a close and old friend of Mewshaw, and where, as it happens, there was a slot and a salary for a visiting writer in residence. From the letters it is clear that Jones's first choice was Iowa. He knew about the place, had visited there in the 1950s when Paul Engle ran the workshop. Engle had tried to hire him then. Now Vance Bourjaily, from the young years in New York when Jones and Styron and Mailer and Bourjaily had been pals, had found himself a niche there, and time and changes had left him the senior fiction writer. The Workshop director was John Leggett, novelist, former editor, and most recently author of *Ross and Tom: Two American Tragedies.* He would be fully aware of who Jones was and, Jones had reason to imagine, somewhat appreciative. There was a question of money. Antrim at FIU was able to offer close to thirty thousand dollars for three quarters —nine months—together with some other benefits. Jones thought Iowa, with a more solid reputation, would be a better base from which to begin his teaching career (if it came to that), but he wanted at least $20,000 from them. As he wrote Mewshaw: "There is still of course the possibility of going to Iowa. I think I could get them up to $20,000 there. It sounds like it from my correspondence with John Leggett."[4]

For whatever reasons the Iowa possibility either did not develop or did not work out. And on January 2, 1974, Jones accepted Harry Antrim's offer to come to FIU.

(Among the Mewshaw letters is, yet again, another wonderfully typical example of Jones's flinty integrity. In the midst of negotiations and questions, Jones pauses to say he has read Mewshaw's latest novel, *The Toll,* in galleys, for which he is prepared to write a blurb. He has praise for the book, in general and detail, but he cannot avoid offering some criticism as well. "My criticisms may sound carping," Jones writes. "But I thought you would want to know exactly what I felt to be less than perfect, so that you could improve on them next time out. All in all, as I said, I think it's a damn good book."5 How could they have imagined Jones would be anything less than a first-rate teacher? And what a kind gesture toward a young, developing novelist—to treat him like a peer, a fellow professional.)

Publication of *Viet Journal* (March 13, 1974) brought Jones and Gloria back to the States for a visit and gave them a chance to find a house on Key Biscayne for the coming academic year and then to continue on to Haiti to celebrate their seventeenth wedding anniversary there before going back to Paris. They were interviewed and photographed while walking on the beach at Cape Florida State Park—he looking trim in a European-style bikini, she windblown and barefoot, armed with a camera.6 Harry Antrim had never worried about the "visibility" of his writer in residence. Jones still had the star quality he had earned with *Eternity*. He could be as visible as he pleased.

Viet Journal was greeted with mixed reviews and fairly limited coverage. It received a good advance notice in *Publishers Weekly*, which described the book as presenting "writing that is gripping, human and far superior to much of the copy that emerged from Indochina during the peak of the war—and a book full of poignant echoes."7 And William C. Cooper in *Library Journal* strongly recommended it: "An interesting, readable, and highly personal account, recommended for public and academic libraries."8 But the "establishment" tone and point of view was that of John Reed. (Curiously, Reed had also served as an enlisted man in the Wolfhound Regiment at Schofield before World War II.) In the *New York Times Book Review*, Reed called it "a disappointment," adding: "Much of it seems to have been written hastily, and without passionate conviction, pro or con, about Vietnam." He concluded that " 'Viet Journal' has to be accounted a pro-Army-in-Vietnam book—one of the few that have been written."9

The Jones family left Paris on July 5, 1974, arriving in New York on July 11. In the following weeks they visited with friends on Long Island (in the area around Sagaponack, where he would buy a house a year later) and on Martha's Vineyard. By early September they were in Miami, settling into their rented house (251 Island Drive, Key Biscayne, Florida) and Jones was ready to go to work. On September 1, he signed a contract as "Visiting Professor and Writer-in-Residence," to run for nine months

(September 6, 1974, to June 12, 1975) at a salary of $27,500, to be paid in twenty biweekly payments of $1,375. On the ninth and tenth he filled out a battery of personnel forms. (In them he listed his rank in the Army as "Sgt.") Money was on his mind, and the immediate cash flow must have seemed uncertain, for, in an unusual gesture for a writer who expects to make any significant income from his writing in the coming year, he took all four of the exemptions he was entitled to on his tax withholding forms. On October 30, he signed a sworn affidavit in the presence of a notary swearing to "support the Constitution of the United States and of the State of Florida."

Florida International University has two campuses now, but at that time it was located in the middle of what had once been Miami International Airport out on the Tamiami Trail. Not far to the west, the Everglades begin. The old runways crisscross the campus, and the airport control tower (which was the original administration building) stands in the center of things. There are several huge new, bunkerlike concrete buildings (one joker calls them examples of Siegfried Line architecture) glittering in the typical hot, bright sunlight. But inside, these buildings have courtyards with fountains and are lush and green with exotic plants and trees. Offices and classrooms were shiny, new (three years old that year), and comfortably air-conditioned. FIU is a "drive-in university." Mewshaw called it "a school for commuters, workies, blacks and Hispanics."[10] It was certainly a place where people of all ages and backgrounds, many of them working people, and many Cuban exiles and people from all the Caribbean countries, came to take courses, which are regularly scheduled until late at night. It is, like the rest of Miami, bilingual, indeed multilingual. Jones had his office and classrooms in the building named Deuxième Maison. Each quarter he taught English 416, Writing Fiction, to between fifteen and twenty officially enrolled students, the class meeting every Wednesday afternoon, from 1:45 to 6:05. During his final twelve-week quarter there he also taught English 499, Special Topics (Fiction Writing), a somewhat more advanced section scheduled to meet on Saturdays from 10:00 A.M. until noon.

His colleagues in the English Department were well pleased with his work and his attitude. He communicated interest and enthusiasm. Jim Hall, a good young poet and story writer in the English Department there, reports that "he so loved college life, the whole idea of being in academe, that he volunteered to work registration, and asked to be included in department meetings and other phases of the game that a visiting writer wouldn't normally go seeking."[11] Like most colleges, FIU has a number of would-be writers among its younger teachers. And as might be expected, they took advantage of Jones's presence to ask him to look at their manuscripts, which he did without complaining and without offering less than his best professional opinion. Hall tells about the fate of a manuscript of his own.

> He looked at a very rough, immature, hastily written detective novel of mine and told me it was immature, rough and seemed to have been hastily written. I seethed, but not long afterwards saw that he'd been right. It was awful. He advised me to roll it through the typewriter again, or to think again about whether or not I wanted to write "that kind of book." The implication was that I didn't know enough about the rough tough real world to do the genre justice. He was probably right.[12]

It was Hall who had been assigned the task of helping Jones get his handgun collection out of France and into the United States, no mean trick considering the elaborate laws and regulations in both countries. Hall came up with a perfectly legal scam involving a gun dealer who would legitimately purchase them and then sell them back.

The acid test of the value of a writer in residence is how he works with students. All the evidence indicates that Jones was an excellent teacher and that his students recognized this and appreciated it. There are any number of pieces about his work at FIU, from that first appearance on the beach in 1974 to a *Miami Herald* write-up, by Andy Rosenblatt ("Miami? He Could Write a Book," July 8, 1975), covering the farewell champagne party his writing students gave him. The most thorough and detailed piece is in *Writer's Yearbook* 1982, by former FIU student David Gelsanliter. It is a rich piece, full of careful quotations and specific examples of Jones's teaching methods. What emerges is a loving portrait of a dedicated and able teacher, one who could also teach "things not taught in textbooks." There's more than a hint of pride there, too, some of the swagger and esprit that "Sgt." Jones would want to cultivate in any outfit he commanded: "Jones knew he was dying when he returned to America after 14 years in Paris," Gelsanliter writes. "It didn't bother him that he

In classroom at Florida International University, holding design for WWII

was writer-in-residence at an obscure university called Florida International, nor that his students were a collection of housewives, the unemployed, retired, a former boxer, a former newspaper reporter or two, several teachers, and a couple of business men."[13]

Sometimes Jones had little surprises for his class. Like the times he brought houseguests (Willie Morris and Irwin Shaw among them) to join the class and participate.

During the last week of February, Jones tried his hand at another kind of teaching, joining the staff (for $1,000 plus expenses) of the annual University of Florida Writers' Conference in Gainesville, directed by novelist Smith Kirkpatrick. There he worked with novelists Andrew Lytle and Harry Crews, poets John Ciardi, John Frederick Nims, and Peter Davison, juvenile writer Joy Anderson, and a group of editors and others from magazines and publishing. Ciardi, a man as tough and as tough-looking as Jones and never famous for delivering casual compliments, liked working with Jones and describes him as "very professional."[14] A newspaper piece, "Would-Be Writers Meet the Real Thing," describes Jones and Ciardi as the real "stars" of the affair.[15] There is correspondence in Texas indicating that Smith Kirkpatrick wanted to hire Jones again for the following year, a rare occurrence except in cases of genuinely popular demand.

In Miami, Jones exerted himself, above and beyond the call of any duty, meeting with all kinds of groups, including high school students, suffering interviews, and enduring panel discussions on any number of topics. He also allowed a photo of himself holding up his index finger to be used in the Miami First campaign of the Greater Miami Chamber of Commerce.

He was now working on a new project for Grosset and Dunlap, an idea which soon became the book *WWII*. In the Proposition, the section which opens *WWII*, Jones explains that the idea that he should write a text for "a picture book of World War II graphic art" came from Art Weithas, the art editor of *Yank*. There was some appeal in this for Jones because he would be given complete freedom to "write anything I wanted to write. . . ." But he couldn't think of anything "new" to say, and he was urgently trying to finish the final volume of his World War II trilogy. Then he looked at the examples of artwork which Weithas had collected and the files in Washington. And he was hooked.

What could have been a kind of coffee table book becomes, as a result of the careful selection of the art work by Weithas and Jones and the full and often highly personal text, a remarkable history of World War II. Much information about Jones's personal life and experiences appears only here, making it as autobiographical as it is historical, and in comments on the artwork, in digressions and asides, Jones is clear and explicit in his view that World War II was a shattering experience for America, that life for Americans could never be the same afterward, that some changes were overdue, but that many were destructive and disastrous to the individual.

But he still had *Whistle* to finish. He told Miami interviewer John Dorschner that he had "two fifths of it done, and it's damn near perfect, in any real literary sense that you want to name."[16]

To students of literature:
    Jim Jones and I went to a fuck film in
New York today—*The Private Afternoons
of Pamela Manna.* We liked it.
    Jones' non-fiction book on World War II is
truly distinguished—elegaic and beautiful,
and will allow him and Gloria to buy a house
on Long Island.
    Whistle will be one of the five or six great
novels in American literature.

                      Willie Morris[17]

•   •   •

WWII appeared in September 1975 to a chorus of mostly favorable notices. *Publishers Weekly* had set the tone for the reaction: "Jones's ruthlessly honest depiction of the young soldier's evolution from Mama's boy to hardened professional—a man numbed by the acceptance of his own death, traumatized forever—is an indelible memorial to the Big War."[18] John Barkham's syndicated review, appearing all over the country, was a rave. "Though this may look like a coffee-table book," Barkham wrote, "with its opulent design and striking graphics by Art Weithas, it represents Jones' best writing in years—war as seen from the viewpoint of 'the hairy, swiftly aging, fighting lower-class soldier.' "[19] Christopher Lehmann-Haupt was equally enthusiastic in the daily *New York Times*: "What Mr. Jones has done . . . is quite simply to make the event come fully alive again."[20] Except that it was not reviewed nearly so *widely* as his novels had been, this was a crest of good response that had not been reached since *The Thin Red Line* in 1962. Only the *Kirkus Reports* was negative about the book as a whole and Jones's contribution to it: "Jones, for his part, provides canny reassessments of battles and pseudoironic macho anecdotes."[21] He had seen a lot worse.

All this would surely help *Whistle* when it came along, as would the extensive and exhausting "media tour" of cities which Grosset and Dunlap arranged for him. Among the cities he visited in September and October were Atlanta, Boston, Chicago, Cincinnati, Cleveland, Detroit, Houston, Los Angeles, Minneapolis, Philadelphia, Pittsburgh, Tampa, and Washington. A sense of how hectic the schedule was is to be found in the one day (Monday, September 29, 1975) schedule at Minneapolis, which has seven full-scale media appointments between breakfast and his flight to the next place. In New York he appeared on television on both *AM America* (August 6) and the *Today Show* (September 10). This was the new world of American publishing with a vengeance, but he was handling this one as well and as easily as he had dealt with the old. In *James Jones: A Friendship*, Willie Morris describes some of the pomp and ceremony associated with the publication of the book.

> When the non-fiction *World War II* came out the publishers gave a lavish party in the Federal City Club in Washington. A sizable portion of the Washington Establishment turned out, including Henry Kissinger, but also large numbers of military brass, generals and admirals on down, all of whom were anxious to meet the author. All this thoroughly amused him. At a small dinner of friends later at the Georgetown Club, it was General Weyand, Commanding General of the U.S. Army, who offered the main toast: "To Pfc Jones, who understood us all."[22]

By the time *WWII* was published, Jones had bought a farmhouse set in an old potato field in Sagaponack, Long Island. And the family had moved there. Now they were close by many old friends, riding high on the waves of good response to *WWII* and to himself. He settled in to finish the long-delayed *Whistle*, and put his Paris apartment on the market, hoping for highly favorable terms. It was sold in November for nearly half a million dollars—this money would become the bulk of his estate.

On February 3, 1976, Jones was able to list his financial assets, not including projected income and not including insurance policies, as $403,185. Against this he listed estimated expenses for 1976, including mortgage, taxes, and insurance, which came to $171,500. He would have to work hard and finish *Whistle* as soon as he could.[23]

That last year and a half on Long Island was a strange one, yet strangely wonderful. All accounts agree that Jones's health was fragile, that he knew it, that he kept his eye on the clock as he wrote. So the essence of it was work, hard lonely hours in his attic study, trying to finish *Whistle*. But in order to do this, to live to go the distance with the book, he would have to pace himself. He needed patience and relaxation more than ever. And then there had to be the sense of perhaps seeing things and the people he loved—Gloria, the children, his close friends—for the last time, the desire to enjoy them while he could, and the perfectly natural wish to be well remembered by them. Add to this the weight of knowing that even if he lived to finish *Whistle* the way he wanted it to be, it was now extremely unlikely that he would live to produce some of the other books he had been dreaming about for many years—the things he had put off until he was really ready for them: the Civil War novel, the Elizabethan novel, the jazz novel, the one or two novels of the new West.[24] And only the year before he had been taking notes and collecting materials on the Cuban exiles in Miami. Surely there might be a good story in that. Well, at least he had enough work to last him even if he ended up living as long as Aunt Mollie. No chance of burning out, running out of material.

But to pace himself, to stay alive for this one, for *Whistle*, he had to take it easy—as much as possible. He *really* couldn't drink anymore—he was down to grapefruit juice on the rocks, though he still liked to be around hearty drinkers. And his salt-free diet was bland and austere to the point of being depressing; nevertheless, as in Paris, he liked to go places where good food was served.

Willie Morris has written the definitive account of those final months on Long Island. The last hundred pages or so of *A Friendship* tell the story eloquently and thoroughly: the beauty of the place, which Jones rejoiced in (and Willie Morris claims is "likely the most lovely terrain in America"); Bobby Van's place and Rick's Bar on Main Street in Bridgehampton; the Golden Nematodes softball team; occasional trips to town with the children for a Mets ball game; cookouts on the beach; New Year's Day, the party and incredible feast at Bobby Van's and all the bowl games; games at home in "Chateau Spud," Monopoly, Risk, chess, and plenty of poker; relaxed dinners there at home with old friends from Paris days or with a

*Sailing with William Styron,
Haiti, 1975*

With his son, Jamie, 1975
(© Gluck-Treaster)

few among the many bona fide celebrities of American culture and show business who loved to come there.

> With coffee Jim would light up one of his cigars and offer them to others. After that there might be some dancing—Sinatra, Bing Crosby, Glen [*sic*] Miller, Fred Astaire—often to the records from World War II.[25]

Morris recalls the Christmas dinner where Jones took the third volume of Shelby Foote's *The Civil War* and read aloud from it the moving excerpts of Oliver Wendell Holmes's speech to the veterans of his old regiment in Keene, New Hampshire, in 1881. But Jones could be happy with quiet solitary things also. Morris says he loved to listen to the *names* when the radio broadcast the college football scores late in autumnal Saturday afternoons. And he was happy in his attic study surrounded by his *things*, the things he had collected and managed to keep over a lifetime.

Willie Morris also tells us about the February 1976 trip he took with Jones and their two sons, Jamie and David, to see the battlefields at Chancellorsville, the Wilderness, and Spotsylvania, Harper's Ferry and Antietam, with a side trip to Charlottesville to see the University of Virginia and Monticello. Morris was writer-in-residence for the *Star*. He wrote a column about the trip for the *Star*: "The Fields of War Become a Cold Companion," February 22, 1976. It was the visit to the quiet fields of Antietam, which "was the bloodiest single day's fighting in the Civil War, some say the bloodiest in the history of mankind until then," that brought from Jones a stunned comment as he viewed the terrain from a little tower: "I don't think men could go any farther than these men did in this battle and still be members of the planet."[26]

E N D

I just loved his voice. It was a cowboy's
voice, like Gary Cooper's.

Gloria Jones[27]

.   .   .

ACCORDING to Morris, Jones was in and out of the hospital a number of
times during his final year and a half on Long Island. On January 14, 1977,
he was admitted to the Southhampton Hospital in a condition serious
enough to merit a story in *The New York Times*. But he recovered and was
soon well enough to go home—to go to work again. His brother, George
W. Jones (Jeff) died in Roanoke that winter at the age of sixty-seven. He,
too, suffered from congestive heart failure. By May Jones was back in the
hospital. According to William Styron, writing in the June 6, 1977, issue of
New York ("A Friend's Farewell to James Jones") : "On Thursday night,
May 5, the doctors told Gloria that Jim was finished. It was a matter of
hours." But Jones hung on until Monday the ninth when, at 7:50 P.M., with
his family and some few close friends nearby, including Morris and Styron,
he died.[28] The obituary in the Tuesday morning *Times* announced that
there would be a memorial service for Jones on May 15 at the Bridgehampton Community House.

Approximately four hundred people came to the forty-minute memorial for Jones that Sunday. Those who were there recollect the back-drop of lilacs, white wild laurel, and apple blossoms, which brought the brightness of the spring day inside. The Alden Whitman piece in the *Times* dutifully noted the presence of various and sundry literary and public figures—Truman Capote, Shana Alexander, Joseph Heller, Peter Matthiessen, Kurt Vonnegut, and Jill Krementz—together with former Mayor John Lindsay and, as well, a contingent from "Long Island Chapter 135 of the Pearl Harbor Survivors' Association."[29] There were eulogies by Irwin Shaw and William Styron. Jones's daughter Kaylie read a favorite poem of his, "Dirge Without Music," by Edna St. Vincent Millay. Rose Styron read Yeats's "The Lake Isle of Innisfree" (which Jones himself, in one of his final acts, had read into his tape recorder at the hospital). Willie Morris closed the service by reading the scene from *From Here to Eternity* of Prewitt playing taps. And finally M/Sgt. Patrick Mastroleo, bugler from the U.S. Army Band, played that final farewell call.

After the service was over, there was a gathering at Jones's house, a party of old, close friends. It was a time for remembering the good times, the good things.

Later that evening, a reporter from the *Charlotte Observer*, an ad-mirer of Jones and his work, called and talked to Irwin Shaw and Willie Morris and a couple of people who had edited the work of Jones. One of them was Burroughs Mitchell, whose statement can be, quite appropri-ately, the last word here: "He did it his way. Jones never cared much whether he was fashionable or unfashionable. He was a marvelous man to work with. Obviously, he knew his own mind and knew what he wanted to do, but he would listen to suggestions."[30]

Before Jones died, he had managed to come within a few pages of finishing *Whistle* according to plan. As Morris explains in the Introductory Note: "*Whistle* was to have had thirty-four chapters. Jones had completed somewhat more than half of Chapter 31 when he again became seriously ill." Morris finished it up, following the outline and instructions. Burroughs Mitchell was called out of retirement to edit it. And on February 22, 1978, a huge black-tie dinner was held at the East Side Armory to honor the novel's publication. Some 270 celebrities and friends of Jones were invited to dine on striped bass, beef Florentine, and citrus mousse, to hear readings (Lauren Bacall read from *The Thin Red Line*, Kevin McCarthy did the bugle scene from *From Here to Eternity*, and Martin Gabel, whom Jones had called "my drinking buddy" in the old days, read from *Whistle*), and to raise toasts. Explaining the intent and meaning of the gathering, Irwin Shaw said: "What we're celebrating is the completion of a massive monument, created by one indomitable man, out of his talent, his persistence, and courage."[31] A great many prominent figures from among the literati were present. Among those listed by *The New York Times* piece about the party, a by no means complete listing, were Susan Sontag, Norman Mailer, Pete Hamill, Joseph Heller, Tommy Thompson, Ralph Ellison, Kurt Vonnegut, Wilfrid Sheed, James T. Farrell, Theodore White, and Budd Schulberg. The *Times* also duly noted the presence of the likes of Woody Allen and Barbara Walters, of Lee Radziwill and Jackie Onassis.

But after that splendid send-off, *Whistle*, a full selection of the Literary Guild and with an excerpt in *Book Digest*, was out there on its own.

In A Note by the Author, dated November 15, 1973, and published with *Whistle*, Jones described the evolution and intention of the World War II trilogy clearly and succinctly. Originally, back in 1947 when he was dealing with Maxwell Perkins, it was all to have been part of one book "from the peacetime Army on through Guadalcanal and New Georgia, to the return of the wounded to the United States." All this was too big to be practical. He wrote *From Here to Eternity*, after which the concept of a trilogy, three clearly separate volumes yet all related parts of a larger whole, began to develop. Jones indicates that by the time he was writing *The Thin Red Line*, he had the trilogy firmly in mind. Because Prewitt had to die in *Eternity* and yet he needed a Prewittlike character throughout the trilogy, he hit upon the idea of changing the names of the characters slightly, together with superficial changes in background, while preserving the inward and spiritual essence, the *truth* of the key characters, under whatever name:

So in *The Thin Red Line* 1st/Sgt. Warden became 1st/Sgt. Welsh, Pvt. Prewitt became Pvt. Witt, Mess/Sgt. Stark became Mess/Sgt. Storm. While remaining the same people as before. In *Whistle* Welsh becomes Mart Winch, Witt becomes Bobby Prell, Storm becomes John Strange.[32]

Jones fails to mention here the transformation of the fourth important character, the one, in fact, most closely modeled on himself and his own personal experiences—Marion Landers, the company clerk, who is directly derived from Cpl. Geoffrey Fife of *The Thin Red Line.*

The full implications of this method remain to be fully examined by the critics. Clearly however, a statement is implied, that there is something almost "eternal" about the three basic figures, that they are, in a sense, more like reincarnations than mere symbols of, say, the perennial enlisted man. They reappear and reenact their destinies, gifted with the same essential character and a new name. They are renewed to live and to suffer again. By the end of *Whistle* they seem to fuse together, to become one composite character. That character dies, and the revels are ended, the story is over.

What happens in *Whistle* is that these four men are shipped home, three with wounds of varying degrees of seriousness and one, Mart Winch, suffering from a congestive heart condition. They are sent to a military hospital in the imaginary town of Luxor, Tennessee, which, as Jones notes, is a blending of the two cities where he stayed on his return from the Pacific in 1943, Memphis and Nashville. Bound together in the family of the company in which they served, they find that though their lives are separate, their fates are somehow inextricable. There is no peace for any one of them except, perhaps, briefly and delusively. There is no understanding or real communication possible between them and the affluent civilians, profiting greatly from the war effort and utterly ignorant of the experiences these walking wounded have endured. The veterans are shocked by "peace" and prosperity at home. They are also shown to be unable to cope with the huge changes in American life, especially the change in morality. The new sexual freedoms confuse and profoundly trouble them all. They are unable to establish lasting relationships with women. Though their wounds may heal, they themselves cannot heal or be well again. In a real sense their lives ended, "they gave up the ghost," in the Pacific. In a sense they are ghosts looking for the peace of a grave.

Jones had written about this, the paradoxes of it, in *WWII*:

It is absolutely true, for example, that when you think, when you *know*, you are going off to die somewhere soon, every day has a special, bright, delicious poignant taste to it that normal times do not have. . . .

Some men like to live like that all the time. Some are actually sorry to come home and see it end. Even those of us who hated it found it exciting, sometimes. That is what the civilian people never understand about their returned soldiers, in any way, Vietnam as well. They cannot understand how we could hate it, and still like it; and they do not realize they have a lot of dead men around them, dead men who are walking around and breathing.[33]

Of the four principals in *Whistle*, three—Prell, Landers, and Strange —find ways to kill themselves, while Winch, who was always closest to death because of his heart condition, goes crazy. He is last seen howling out of his hallucinatory memories from the barred windows of a psychiatric hospital. The last image of the whole book is Mess/Sgt. Strange, quietly dropping off a troopship bound for Europe, treading water in the ocean, waiting to freeze or drown.

It is a bleak story and a tragic one, yet it is not unrelieved. Up to the end, including the last three chapters which are told synoptically in the form he left them, there is all the energy, vitality, even the broad humor and richness of observed detail that one associates with the best of Jones's fiction. The triumph of the trilogy is that its created power finally overcomes even its own negative statement. It is, thus, truly tragic, not simply nihilistic.

Technically there is one original and interesting variation which strengthens the novel. The first chapter, and that chapter only, is told collectively in the first person plural by anonymous members of the old company who are already in the United States, in various hospitals, establishing the information that the four major characters are coming home. After that, the rest of the novel is told by an omniscient narrator speaking in "colloquial forms." This device, of course, serves to create a sense of the company as a loving and concerned family, but in a narrative sense it adds something more. In a serious, functional sense it isolates the *source* of the language of the novel—style, grammar, syntax, idiom. And simultaneously it *justifies* language. The reader is given to understand that it is coming from a collective consciousness, perception, and verbal capacity. Moreover this simple, yet powerfully effective device makes it possible to reconsider other, earlier works which were composed in "colloquial forms." Perhaps if he had used an introduction or prologue establishing the consciousness of a collective narrator in *Some Came Running* or *Go to the Widow-Maker*, there would have been less critical misunderstanding of those works.

Then the reviews came in. Prior to publication date, *Publishers*

Jones's brother, George W. Jones

Portrait by Ole Brask

Weekly had given the book a strongly positive notice: "It's all unmistakably and uncomfortably real."[34] Following publication, the coverage was widespread and thorough, since most reviewers felt that it was an appropriate occasion to reexamine Jones's career and his place in our nation's literature. In *The Nation* Leonard Kriegel, depicting Jones as bearing out Philip Rahv's division of American writers into "palefaces" and "redskins," described Jones as "the very model of a redskin writer." After treating some faults and weaknesses, Kriegel finally offered praise: "With all that he could not do as a writer, Jones possessed a command of the novelistic situation that few contemporary writers possess."[35] In *Newsweek* Peter S. Prescott, though he pointed out that neither in *Whistle* nor elsewhere had Jones written anything "even remotely convincing about women," was positive in his appreciation of the book. "Politics, at least of the kind practiced within the Army, have always been Jones's strength. He understood better than anyone the mind of the professional enlisted man and the elliptical processes by which favors are bartered and officers outflanked, the tricks by which the Army's bureaucracy can be exploited."[36] Frank Trippett of *Time* was negative. "The rushed bumpy narrative seems less a novel than an outline."[37] John Aldridge, reviewing it for the *New York Times Book Review*, while not backing off from the views he had expressed in his savaging of *The Merry Month of May*, gave the novel serious and basically favorable attention, and at some length. "Jones may not be recognized as a literary artist of the first rank," Aldridge maintained. "But he was a powerful naturalistic chronicler of certain essential responses of men at war, and he had a gift of being absolutely honest about what he felt and thought."[38]

Thomas R. Edwards, writing in the *New York Review of Books*, dealt seriously with a technical problem Jones had always wrestled with: the creation of a language for basically inarticulate men. He concluded, however, that the novel was "a very badly written book" and that Jones was "a minor novelist, one with a single subject and a limited control of his craft."[39]

In the *Saturday Review* it was a young novelist, Tim O'Brien, author of the recently published Vietnam novel, *Going After Cacciato*, who walked a kind of tightrope of appreciation and criticism. Allowing that there "are awkward passages and awkward scenes in the novel, particularly those that involve women," he nevertheless noted that there "are also jewels of storytelling."[40]

But if the reception in New York was mixed, this was not the case nationwide. The reaction of reviewers almost everywhere else was strongly positive. They took and understood *Whistle* for what it was, thus demonstrating the oddly parochial, curiously *regional* quality New York culture had managed to acquire. In the *Chicago Tribune*, Vietnam author Philip Caputo argued that "Jones ought to be taken very seriously because no one has written about the soldier and his world more accurately and eloquently."[41] Perhaps the straightforward review for *Library Journal*, by Bruce M. Firestone of Clemson, may be fairly taken as exemplary of the national critical response to the book: "*Whistle* may not be equal in sheer writing power to *From Here to Eternity*, but it is a strong, carefully crafted novel, one which paints a vivid and often harrowing portrait of men who return home from war only to find that the war rages on in their minds."[42]

Seymour Krim wrote a fine essay review of Willie Morris' *James Jones* and with it a reconsideration of Jones as man and artist. Krim sees the ending of *Whistle* (and thus the whole trilogy, the center of all Jones's work) as almost exclusively negative. "His last novel, *Whistle*," Krim concludes, "makes it clear that he could no longer see the purpose of life in our time."[43] Certainly that inference can be derived from the story of *Whistle*. But from the larger story of the trilogy, in which characters die or simply vanish into thin air with the ending of the particular story they inhabit, one can infer that Jones believed that there is some essential energy, some kind of continuity, a sort of resurrection of the very essence of character which transcends the limits of individual experience and even identity.

Scholars and critics may choose to wrestle with that problem in the future. Certainly it is no longer a problem for Jones, whose books and characters live on after him. He was already beyond all power to praise or blame, to wound or to bless, when *Whistle* appeared.

NOTES

•   •   •

PREFACE

1. To George W. (Jeff) Jones, November 3, 1942. James Jones Papers, Collection of American Literature, the Beinecke Rare Book and Manuscript Library, Yale University. Hereinafter the Yale Collection of American Literature will be referred to as YCAL.
2. Shelby Foote to George P. Garrett, November 8, 1982.
3. Creativity & Mental Health Panel (typescript transcription), Tape 3, p. 9, June 3, 1975. Humanities Research Center, University of Texas at Austin.
4. Garrett interview with John Aldridge, Ann Arbor, Michigan, January 1983.
5. *Viet Journal* (New York: Delacorte Press, 1974), 249.

PART ONE: A REAPPRAISAL

1. To Burroughs Mitchell, March 18, 1950. YCAL and Princeton University Library.
2. James R. Giles, *James Jones* (Boston: Twayne Publishers, 1981), 10.

3. Budd Schulberg, *The Four Seasons of Success* (Garden City, N.Y.: Doubleday, 1972), 14.

4. To Burroughs Mitchell, October 23, 1949. YCAL and Princeton University Library.

5. To Burroughs Mitchell, November 27, 1950. YCAL and Princeton University Library.

6. Quoted by Michael S. Lasky in "James Jones Has Come Home to Whistle," *Writers' Digest* 56 (October 1976), 23.

7. John Leggett, *Ross and Tom: Two American Tragedies* (New York: Simon and Schuster, 1974), 434.

8. To Burroughs Mitchell, December 14, 1956. YCAL and Princeton University Library.

9. To James Jones, December 14, 1956. YCAL.

10. Burroughs Mitchell, *The Education of an Editor* (New York: Doubleday, 1980), 73.

11. "From Eternity to Here," *Newsweek*, January 13, 1958, 89.

12. Joan Didion, "Goodbye, Gentleman-ranker," *Esquire* 88 (October 1977), 55, 60.

13. "The Good Life and Jim Jones," *Life* 42 (February 11, 1957), 83.

14. Untitled manuscript, YCAL.

15. To Carl Jones, March 29, 1962. Humanities Research Center.

16. Granville Hicks, "The Shorter and Better Jones," *Saturday Review* 42 (January 10, 1959), 12.

17. "The Writer Speaks: A Conversation Between James Jones and Leslie Hanscom" (1962), in *James Jones: A Checklist*, compiled by John R. Hopkins (Detroit: Bruccoli Clark/Gale Research, 1974), 14.

18. To Mrs. Dorothy Chatman, May 10, 1959. Humanities Research Center.

19. To William Styron, December 2, 1959. Humanities Research Center.

20. Maurice Dolbier, "What NBA Means to Some Past Winners," *New York Herald Tribune*, March 1, 1959, 11.

21. To Michael Mewshaw, April 18, 1974. Humanities Research Center.

22. To Norman Mailer, March 5, 1956. Humanities Research Center.

23. To Mr. and Mrs. Guy Haish, November 23, 1932. YCAL.

24. To Jeff Jones, January 28, 1943. YCAL.

25. To Jeff Jones, May 22, 1943. YCAL.

26. To Burroughs Mitchell, April 7, 1949. YCAL.

27. *WWII*, 150.

28. *WWII*, 151.

29. "Story Behind the Book: 'A Touch of Danger,'" *Publishers Weekly* 203 (May 7, 1973), 39.

30. Hugh Moffett, "Aging Heavy of the Paris Expatriates," *Life* 63 (August 4, 1967), 34.
31. To Jeff Jones, May 22, 1940. YCAL.
32. To Maxwell Perkins, October 30, 1946. YCAL and Princeton University Library.
33. To Maxwell Perkins, March 16, 1947. YCAL and Princeton University Library.
34. To Burroughs Mitchell, February 16, 1951. YCAL and Princeton University Library.
35. To M. J. Lasky, undated. YCAL.
36. To William Styron, May 23, 1960. YCAL.
37. "The Writer Speaks," 10.
38. *Ernest Hemingway: Selected Letters 1917–1961*, ed. Carlos Baker (New York: Scribner's, 1981), 721.
39. To Maxwell Perkins, October 21, 1946. YCAL and Princeton University Library.
40. To John Hall Wheelock, December 9, 1947. YCAL.
41. James Jones, "Letter Home: Sons of Hemingway," *Esquire* 60 (December 1963), 34.
42. To Burroughs Mitchell, October 3, 1961. Princeton University Library.
43. Herman Gollob to Jones, September 16, 1964. Humanities Research Center.
44. To Walter J. Minton, August 9, 1956. Humanities Research Center.
45. To Walter J. Minton, August 19, 1956. Humanities Research Center.
46. Norman Mailer, "The Big Bite," *Esquire* 59 (June 1963), 23.
47. To Richard P. Adams, May 4, 1955. Humanities Research Center.
48. To Mary Ann Jones, January 8, 1946. YCAL.
49. *The Overseas Family* (November 11, 1960), 32.
50. "Aging Heavy," 34.
51. "Too Much Symbolism," *The Nation* 176 (May 2, 1953), 369.
52. *Viet Journal*, 257.
53. John Hall Wheelock to James Jones, January 5, 1951. YCAL.

PART TWO: BOY TO MAN

1. To Aunt Mollie Haish, April 15, 1934. YCAL.
2. To Mrs. Frederick W. Tahse, April 28, 1956. Humanities Research Center.
3. "James Jones: Another 'Eternity'?," *Newsweek*, November 23, 1953, 104.
4. *Ford Times* 49 (March 1957), 53.
5. *Robinson Argus* (November 11, 1954), 3.
6. *Twentieth Century Authors (First Supplement): A Biographical Dictionary*

of Modern Literature, ed. Stanley J. Kunitz and Vineta Colby (New York: H. W. Wilson, 1955), 500–501.

7. *Illinois: Guide & Gazetteer* (Chicago: Rand McNally, 1969), 449.

8. A. B. C. Whipple, "James Jones and His Angel," *Life* 30 (May 7, 1951), 143.

9. "The Writer Speaks," 16.

10. To Burroughs Mitchell, February 23, 1948. YCAL and Princeton University Library.

11. To Jeff Jones, May 28, 1941. YCAL.

12. To Burroughs Mitchell, November 12, 1946. YCAL and Princeton University Library.

13. To Jeff Jones, August 21, 1940. YCAL.

14. To Jeff Jones, May 28, 1941. YCAL.

15. To Jeff Jones, May 7, 1941. YCAL.

16. To Jeff Jones, August 21, 1940. YCAL.

17. Willie Morris, *James Jones: A Friendship* (Garden City, N.Y.: Doubleday, 1978), 32.

18. *The Ice-Cream Headache and Other Stories*, 195.

19. *Ice-Cream Headache*, 203.

20. *Ice-Cream Headache*, 216.

21. *Ice-Cream Headache*, 200–201.

22. *Ice-Cream Headache*, 168.

23. *Ice-Cream Headache*, 165–66.

24. *The New York Times*, April 21, 1968, 52.

25. To Burroughs Mitchell, May 6, 1948. YCAL and Princeton University Library.

26. Nelson W. Aldrich, Jr., "James Jones," in *Writers at Work: The Paris Review Interviews, Third Series* (New York: Viking Press, 1967), 240. Interview originally published in *Paris Review* 5 (Autumn–Winter 1958–1959).

27. David Slavitt to George Garrett, September 9, 1982.

28. Arthur Goodfriend, "The Cognoscenti Abroad—II: James Jones's Paris," *Saturday Review* 52 (February 1, 1969), 37.

29. "Cognoscenti Abroad," 36.

30. June 3, 1975, typed transcription of tape recording, tape 2, 13. Humanities Research Center.

31. Tape 4, 1.

32. To Jeff Jones, December 8, 1939. YCAL.

33. To Jeff Jones, May 28, 1940.

34. Garrett conversation with Joe Brown.

35. To Burroughs Mitchell, November 12, 1946. YCAL and Princeton University Library.

36. *Viet Journal*, 242–43.

37. To Jeff Jones, May 7, 1941. YCAL.

38. Untitled article in *Attacks of Taste*, ed. Evelyn B. Byrne and Otto M. Penzler (New York: Gotham Book Mart, 1971), 26–27.

39. "James Jones, 1921–1977," *The New York Times*, June 12, 1977, 3.

40. *Commentary* 66 (April 4, 1978), 91.

41. "Good-bye, Gentleman-ranker," *Esquire* 88 (October 1977), 60.

42. Dr. Ramon Jones to James Jones, December 31, 1940. Beinecke Library.

43. To Burroughs Mitchell, March 29, 1950. YCAL and Princeton University Library.

44. *WWII*, 70–71.

45. To Burroughs Mitchell, May 5, 1949. YCAL and Princeton University Library.

46. Dr. Ramon Jones to James Jones, March 3, 1941. Humanities Research Center.

47. YCAL. Personal notebook.

48. Dr. Jones to Illinois Military Area, February 25, 1942. Humanities Research Center.

49. "Suicide Is Verdict in Dr. Ramon Jones Death," *Robinson Argus* (March 19, 1942), 1.

50. James Jones to Mary Ann Jones, March 22, 1942. YCAL.

51. To Burroughs Mitchell, October 6, 1948. YCAL and Princeton University Library.

52. To Burroughs Mitchell, March 22, 1950. YCAL.

53. *Viet Journal*, 1–2.

54. To Aunt Mollie Haish, January 20, 1948. YCAL.

55. Garrett interview with Gloria Jones. February 1983.

56. *WWII*, 25.

57. *WWII*, 40.

58. *WWII*, 41.

59. James Jones to Jeff Jones, October 26, 1942. YCAL.

60. To Jeff Jones, November 3, 1942. YCAL.

61. YCAL. Untitled diary notebook.

62. Quoted in Herbert Christian Merillat, *Guadalcanal Remembered* (New York: Dodd, Mead, 1982), 285.

63. *WWII*, 71.

64. YCAL. 1950s notebook untitled.

65. John Miller, Jr., *Guadalcanal: The First Offensive* (Washington, D. C.: Department of the Army, 1949), 258–59.

66. *The First Offensive*, 264.

67. *The First Offensive*, 267. This incident, with others described by Miller, was witnessed by Jones and later used in *The Thin Red Line*.

68. Samuel B. Griffith II, *The Battle for Guadalcanal* (Philadelphia: Lippincott, 1963), 236.

69. *The First Offensive*, 275–76.

70. *WWII*, 53.

71. YCAL.

72. To Jeff Jones, February 19, 1943. YCAL.

73. YCAL.

74. *The Saturday Evening Post* 236 (March 30, 1963), 64–67.

75. To Burroughs Mitchell, April 7, 1949. YCAL and Princeton University Library.

76. YCAL.

77. YCAL.

78. YCAL.

79. YCAL.

80. YCAL.

81. To Marshall Wingfield, March 6, 1951. YCAL.

82. To Jeff Jones, June 3, 1944. YCAL.

PART THREE: BEGINNING

1. To Burroughs Mitchell, August 16, 1949. YCAL and Princeton University Library.

2. To Burroughs Mitchell, April 22, 1956. Humanities Research Center and Princeton University Library.

3. To Maxwell Perkins, March 16, 1947. YCAL and Princeton University Library.

4. To Jeff Jones, May (?), 1941. YCAL.

5. *Education of an Editor,* 57.

6. *Education of an Editor*, 63.

7. Seymour Krim, "Versions of Jones" (Review of Willie Morris, *James Jones: A Friendship*) *The Nation* 227 (October 28, 1978), 448.

8. Ned Brown to James Jones, January 30, 1953. YCAL.

9. Shelby Foote to George Garrett, December 10, 1982.

10. To John Hall Wheelock, October 4, 1950. YCAL.

11. To Burroughs Mitchell, November 8, 1950. YCAL and Princeton University Library.

12. *A Friendship*, 53.

13. "James Jones and His Angel," *Life* 30 (May 7, 1951), 152.

14. *A Friendship*, 53.

15. Undated copy, to Lowney Handy, signed Jules Goldstone. YCAL.
16. To Burroughs Mitchell, February 22, 1951. YCAL.
17. David Ray to George Garrett, December 4, 1982.
18. To Burroughs Mitchell, June 28, 1950. YCAL and Princeton University Library.
19. In the YCAL, there is a copy of a letter from Maxwell Aley to Thaddeus Culmer of Robinson, Illinois, thanking Culmer and his wife for sending James Jones to the Aleys. "He is something pretty special," Aley writes, "and he definitely has a future as a writer." Jones's relations with agents over the years are, at this point, complex and confusing to follow. At first, at least, he does not seem to have used agents at all except for occasional one-shot projects. He dealt directly with Scribner's, and Burroughs Mitchell acted in part as an agent for him, helping him place some of his stories in magazines. Among the literary agents he seems to have dealt with in specific matters are Horace Morewood, Marian Ives, Jacques Chambrun, Paul Reynolds, Scott Meredith, both Diarmuid Russell and Henry Volkening, separately, Phyllis Jackson, and Perry Knowlton. It was Phyllis Jackson of Ashley Famous Artists who arranged the details of the Dell Contract of 1964 when James left Scribner's. Scribner's had handled all the foreign rights for Jones until 1961 when Hope Lekesche took charge. Ned Brown of MCA handled the film rights for *From Here to Eternity* and *Some Came Running* and also arranged some screenwriting gigs for him. In the early 1960s Jones dropped Brown and hired Alain Bernheim.
20. To Dr. Carl Stroven, February 4, 1946. YCAL.
21. To Maxwell Perkins, February 10, 1946. YCAL and Princeton University Library.
22. Undated memo (in context obviously early 1946) by Burroughs Mitchell. YCAL. See also *The Education of an Editor*, 57–58.
23. Maxwell Perkins to James Jones, February 16, 1946. YCAL and Princeton University Library.
24. To Maxwell Perkins, February 17, 1946. YCAL and Princeton University Library.
25. *Editor to Author: The Letters of Maxwell E. Perkins*, ed. John Hall Wheelock (New York: Scribner's, 1950), 273–74, 295–99.
26. Harvey Breit, *The Writer Observed* (Cleveland: World Publishing Co., 1956), 180.
27. To Maxwell Perkins, March 4, 1946. YCAL and Princeton University Library.
28. To Maxwell Perkins, March 16, 1947. Princeton University Library.
29. To Maxwell Perkins, April 9, 1946. Princeton University Library.
30. *Education of an Editor*, 58.

31. *Education of an Editor*, 58.
32. To Burroughs Mitchell, April 7, 1949. Princeton University Library.
33. To Burroughs Mitchell, April 25, 1949. Princeton University Library.
34. Merle Miller to Burroughs Mitchell, March 23, 1948. Princeton University Library.
35. Bentley Historical Museum (University of Michigan), Box 3, Article Files 1933–1959.
36. To Burroughs Mitchell, November 8, 1949. YCAL and Princeton University Library.
37. John Hall Wheelock to James Jones, December 5, 1949. YCAL.
38. To Robert E. Harris, September 8, 1950. YCAL.
39. To Horace S. Manges, November 27, 1950. YCAL and Princeton University Library.
40. To Burroughs Mitchell, November 13, 1950. YCAL and Princeton University Library.
41. To Burroughs Mitchell, December 24, 1950. YCAL and Princeton University Library.
42. Ray Bell to Harry Cohn, March 13, 1951. YCAL.
43. *New York Herald Tribune*, February 25, 1951, 7.
44. Robert F. Kingery, *Library Journal* 76 (March 1, 1951), 409.
45. *New York Times*, February 25, 1951, 5.
46. "This Man's Army," *Atlantic Monthly* 187 (March 1951), 83.
47. "The Real Enemy Is Hard to Find," *Saturday Review* 34 (February 24, 1951), 11–12.
48. *Washington Post*, February 25, 1951, 7B.
49. *Life* 30 (April 16, 1951), 40.
50. *Harper's* 202 (June 1951), 67–70.
51. *Kenyon Review* 13 (Summer 1951), 529.
52. "Minority Report" (March 17, 1951), 254.
53. *Commentary* 12 (September 1951), 253.
54. *New Republic* 138 (January 27, 1958), 16.
55. "Fiction of the Second World War," *College English* 17 (January 1956), 201.
56. "A Second Look at *From Here to Eternity*," *College English* 17 (January 1956), 208.
57. Peter G. Jones, *War and the Novelist: Appraising the American War Novel* (Columbia, Mo.: University of Missouri Press, 1976), 42.
58. *Nashville Tennessean*, February 10, 1951.
59. *Dallas Morning News*, February 10, 1951.
60. *Providence Journal*, February 17, 1951.
61. To Mrs. Burroughs Mitchell, October 4, 1950. YCAL.

62. To Shelby Foote, June 8, 1959. Courtesy of Shelby Foote.

63. *A Friendship*, 82–92.

64. *A Friendship*, 91.

65. *Newsweek*, November 23, 1953, 102–103.

66. Shelby Foote to George Garrett, December 19, 1982.

67. *Mailer: A Biography* (New York: Empire Books, 1982), 134–38.

68. Patricia Bosworth, *Montgomery Clift: A Biography* (New York: Harcourt Brace Jovanovich, 1978), 200–201.

69. Montgomery Clift to James Jones, December 4, 1952. YCAL.

70. *The Nation* 227 (October 28, 1978), 448.

71. Novelist and poet Richard Elman, himself a protégé of Burroughs Mitchell and, in fact, the subject of a chapter in *The Education of an Editor*, recalls meeting Jones and Gloria at a party given by Mitchell. "I had the feeling that they would be just as comfortable talking with Frank Sinatra as with me." Jones seems to have impressed most people as being larger than he really was. Elman, a large man, was surprised at how *small* Jones was, but sensed the complex physical impression Jones created. "One of the strongest impressions I had, when I first met him," Elman remembers, "was how small he was. But he seemed like a small giant—big shoulders and stocky and his head was large. He was wearing a suit that night with padded shoulders. And he had a kind of swagger." Conversation of the author with Richard Elman, July 1982, Bennington, Vermont.

72. *Newsweek*, November 23, 1953, 106.

73. David Ray to George Garrett, February 13, 1983.

74. To Horace S. Manges, March 8, 1954. YCAL.

75. To Burroughs Mitchell, September 23, 1949. YCAL.

76. To Burroughs Mitchell, November 8, 1950. YCAL and Princeton University Library.

77. To Burroughs Mitchell, July 13, 1954. YCAL. Former Scribner's editor Donald Hutter recalls that he left the manuscript of *The Pistol* on a Connecticut commuter train (a catastrophe in those pre-Xerox days), chased the train to New Haven, where he recovered the manuscript. And he never told anyone about that near disaster until now. (Garrett interview with Donald Hutter, February 17, 1983.)

78. To Seymour Krim, October 26, 1961. Humanities Research Center.

79. *Newsweek*, January 13, 1958, 89.

80. "Writers' Concentration Camp," *Writers' Digest* 35 (September 1955), 30–34.

81. *London Magazine* 5 (1958), 35–41.

82. *The Nation* 186 (February 8, 1958), 123.

83. *Chicago* 5 (September 1956), 22–27.

84. To Kenneth B. Hawkins, September 8, 1956. Humanities Research Center.

85. *Chicago* 5 (September 1956), 27.

86. To Kenneth B. Hawkins. Humanities Research Center.

87. *Robinson Argus*, December 6, 1956, 1.

88. David Ray to George Garrett, February 13, 1983.

89. To Burroughs Mitchell, August 20, 1954. YCAL.

90. James Jones, "Living in a Trailer," *Holiday* 12 (July 1952), 76.

91. "Living in a Trailer," 81.

92. *Writers at Work*, 240.

93. "Too Much Symbolism," *The Nation* 176 (May 2, 1953), 369.

94. "Too Much Symbolism," 369.

95. To Burroughs Mitchell, September 12, 1956. Princeton University Library.

96. To Norman Mailer, May 3, 1955. Humanities Research Center.

97. "By Sex Obsessed," *New York Times*, January 12, 1958, 32.

98. *Chicago Tribune*, January 12, 1958, 3.

99. *Time*, January 13, 1958, 96.

100. *Library Journal* 83 (January 1, 1958), 79.

101. *The New Yorker* 33 (January 18, 1958), 94, 96.

102. William J. Smith, "The Innocence and Sincerity of a Regular Guy," *Commonweal* 67 (February 7, 1958), 491.

103. *Atlantic Monthly* 201 (January 1958), 78.

104. *New Leader* 41 (January 27, 1958), 20–22.

105. *Daily Variety* (December 26, 1956) ran a story, evidently "leaked" or "planted" by Jones's film agent, Ned Brown, headlined: "JAMES JONES ASKING $1,000,000 FOR FILM RIGHTS TO NEW NOVEL," 3.

106. "Creativity and Mental Health" (June 3, 1975) Tape 3, 9.

107. *A Friendship*, 81.

108. Garrett conversation with Kenneth Rosen, July 1982.

109. "Jones," *Contemporary Novelists*, ed. James Vinson (New York: St. Martin's Press, 1972), 693.

110. Lee Butcher, "Me and Mr. Jones," *Writers' Digest* 56 (October 1976), 25.

111. "The Shorter and Better Jones," *Saturday Review* 42 (January 10, 1959), 12.

112. *Commonweal* 69 (February 6, 1959), 500.

113. Writing to his friend Shelby Foote, 8 June 1959, Jones said: "I wanted to try my hand at a little symbolic novel in the manner of the French. It's really no more than a breather. It was fun to write, and easy, because it didn't really attempt to attack any of the really bigger problems."

PART FOUR: PARIS YEARS

1. Note in Jones's hand on reverse side of a formal place card which is labeled "Monsieur Jones." Humanities Research Center.

2. To Burroughs Mitchell, March 11, 1964. Humanities Research Center and Princeton University Library.

3. *A Friendship*, 93–155.

4. "Aging Heavy," 34.

5. Kenneth MacLeish, "Île de la Cité, Birthplace of Paris," *National Geographic* 133 (May 1968), 717.

6. "Cognoscenti Abroad," 36–38.

7. "Cognoscenti Abroad," 36.

8. Special Note, *The Thin Red Line* (New York: Scribner's, 1962), ix.

9. *Writers at Work*, 247–48.

10. *New York Herald Tribune*, September 9, 1962, 1.

11. *New York Times*, September 9, 1962, 1.

12. "Some Notes on Recent American Fiction," in *The American Novel Since World War II*, ed. Marcus Klein (Greenwich, Conn.: Fawcett, 1969), 159–74. As cited and quoted by Giles, *James Jones*, 218.

13. Norman Mailer, "Some Children of the Goddess," *Esquire* 60 (July 1963), 63.

14. *War and the Novelist*, 172.

15. "Recent Fiction, Part 1: 'What Film Gets Good . . . ,'" *The Nation* 195 (November 17, 1962), 331.

16. Garrett interview with Jon Manchip White, November 1982.

17. "Dreams and Destruction," *Newsweek*, June 1, 1964, 83.

18. To Burroughs Mitchell, November 1963. Princeton University Library.

19. To Burroughs Mitchell, September 2, 1963. Princeton University Library.

20. To Burroughs Mitchell, October 10, 1963. Princeton University Library.

21. "Dreams and Destruction," 83.

22. To Burroughs Mitchell, May 28, 1963. Princeton University Library.

23. Burroughs Mitchell to James Jones, June 4, 1963. Princeton University Library.

24. To Burroughs Mitchell, June 10, 1963. Princeton University Library.

25. Gloria Jones to Burroughs Mitchell, March 1, 1964. Princeton University Library.

26. To Burroughs Mitchell, October 10, 1964. Princeton University Library.

27. To Burroughs Mitchell, November 10, 1964. Princeton University Library.

28. To Burroughs Mitchell, November 19, 1964. Humanities Research Center and Princeton University Library.

29. Garrett interview February 1983. Former editor wishes to preserve anonymity.

30. "Cognoscenti Abroad," 38.

31. YCAL. Untitled notes on *Widow-Maker*.

32. Dannye Romine, "Jones Will Be Remembered from Here to Eternity," *Charlotte Observer*, May 15, 1977, 2G.

33. *Commonweal* 86 (June 30, 1967), 427.
34. *Library Journal* 92 (April 1, 1967), 1509.
35. *New York Times*, April 2, 1967, 5, 50.
36. "The Jones Boy Forever," *Atlantic Monthly* 219 (June 1967), 68.
37. "The Jones Boy Forever," 72.
38. *Library Journal* 96 (January 15, 1971), 207.
39. *New York Times*, February 14, 1971, 7.
40. "Stranger Than Truth," *Hudson Review* 24 (Summer 1971), 361.
41. *Mediterranean Review*, Winter 1972, 47.
42. *Newsweek*, February 15, 1971, 88.
43. "Twosomes and Threesomes in Gray Paree," *Saturday Review* 54 (February 13, 1971), 23.
44. To Robert W. Stallman, May 18, 1959. Humanities Research Center.
45. Ihab Hassan, *Contemporary American Literature, 1945–1972: An Introduction* (New York: Frederick Ungar, 1973), 66.
46. "Cognoscenti Abroad," 36. Arthur Goodfriend writes that the chef was a veteran of Rommel's Afrika Korps.
47. "Sons of Hemingway," 28, 30, 34, 40, 44.
48. "Cognoscenti Abroad," 37.
49. Matthew J. Bruccoli to George Garrett, May 20, 1983.
50. "Sons of Hemingway," 24.
51. Review of *The Dark Side of Genius: The Life of Alfred Hitchcock, New York Times Book Review*, March 6, 1983, 32.
52. To Burroughs Mitchell, June 21, 1961. Princeton University Library.
53. *New York Times*, "Arts and Leisure," March 6, 1983, 4.
54. "Cognoscenti Abroad," 38.
55. To Michael Mewshaw, October 17, 1973. Humanities Research Center.
56. For an excellent and thorough interview with Jones—concerning, among other things, his decision to return to America—see Ira Simmons, "James Jones: Coming Home," *Courier-Journal & Times* (Louisville), September 15, 1974, E6.

PART FIVE: HOME TO WHISTLE
1. To Michael Mewshaw, September 14, 1973. Humanities Research Center.
2. Interview with James Jones by John Dorschner, *Tropic* magazine [*Miami Herald*], January 5, 1975, 18.
3. Michael Mewshaw, "James Jones, Another Side," *Nation* 226 (April 8, 1978), 407.
4. To Michael Mewshaw, December 5, 1973. Humanities Research Center.
5. To Michael Mewshaw, November 9, 1973. Humanities Research Center. Again

and again in his correspondence with other writers who were friends and whose work he admired, Jones does not hesitate to offer serious and constructive criticism of their work; and he expected to receive the same honest treatment at their hands. As he told Shelby Foote after offering criticism of *Love in a Dry Season* and *Follow Me Down*, and enclosing a presentation copy of *Eternity* for Foote: "I hope I haven't given offense. If I have, lets keep it friendly: You are hereby authorized to tear apart *Eternity* and present me the pieces. . . ." April 9, 1952. (Courtesy of Shelby Foote.)

6. Louise Montgomery, "Author Comes Home: From Paris to Key Biscayne," *Miami Herald*, February 23, 1974, 1B.

7. *Publishers Weekly*, February 18, 1974, 70.

8. *Library Journal*, April 15, 1974, 1111.

9. *New York Times*, March 17, 1974, 4.

10. "Another Side," 407.

11. Jim Hall to George Garrett, November 25, 1982.

12. Jim Hall to Garrett, November 25, 1982.

13. David Gelsanliter, "Remembering James Jones," *Writers' Yearbook 1982*, 74. See also Patricia Burstein, "Author James Jones Tries to Impart the Mysteries of Creative Writing," *People* 3 (May 12, 1975), 44–46.

14. Garrett interview with John Ciardi, November 1982.

15. Al Burt, "Would-Be Writers Meet the Real Thing," *Miami Herald*, March 2, 1975, 6F.

16. "James Jones," *Tropic*, January 5, 1975, 22.

17. Willie Morris, A Memo, January 16, 1975 (written on Hotel Blackstone, N.Y. stationery). Humanities Research Center.

18. *Publishers Weekly* 207 (June 23, 1975), 75.

19. John Barkham's review appeared in such newspapers as the *Cincinnati Post*, August 30, 1975, and the Toledo *Blade*, August 31, 1975. Clippings can be found in James Jones Archives of Humanities Research Center.

20. "James Jones on How It Was," *New York Times*, September 10, 1975, 26.

21. *Kirkus Reports*, August 15, 1975. Humanities Research Center.

22. *A Friendship*, 206.

23. Papers in Humanities Research Center.

24. In 1958 something of the size of Jones's hopes and intentions was a matter of public knowledge; for in the in-depth *Newsweek* piece, "From Eternity to Here," a long-term, serious program is described: "Jones has already laid out, in meticulous card files, themes and characters for eleven more novels. His range of proposed subjects is ambitious, to say the least. 'The next one, probably, will be laid in France and be about a French jazz musician, now dead. Then I'd like to do a modern Western, then a novel set in Florida, then one

about New York and one about Hollywood.' " (*Newsweek*, January 13, 1958, 90.) Earlier, in 1955, columnist Bob Considine quoted Jones outlining a list of future projects. " 'I've got the psychiatrist novel, the Florida fishing novel, the modern Western, the short one (to prove I can), the home front novel, the combat novel that will follow where 'Eternity' stopped, the New York literary novel, the Hollywood novel, of course, the Kentucky novel. . . . Oh I can't tell them all, any more than I can reveal to you the name of my next.' " *Cincinnati Enquirer*, October 24, 1955, 18. Clipping in Humanities Research Center.

25. *A Friendship*, 180.

26. *A Friendship*, 234.

27. Quoted in *The New York Times*, February 23, 1978, C-15.

28. *New York Times*, May 10, 1977, 36. See also William Styron, *This Quiet Dust and Other Writings* (New York: Random House, 1982), 267–70.

29. Alden Whitman, "James Jones Hailed by Friends/At a Memorial Service on L.I.," *New York Times*, May 16, 1977, 33. See also "Letters," *New York* 10 (June 20, 1977), 5; *A Friendship*, 250–53; "Remembering James Jones," 74.

30. "Jones Will Be Remembered," 2G.

31. *New York Times*, February 23, 1975, C-15.

32. A Note by the Author, *Whistle*, xx.

33. *WWII*, 54.

34. *Publishers Weekly* 213 (January 16, 1978), 91.

35. "From the Infected Zones," *Nation* 226 (April 8, 1978), 405–406.

36. "Warriors Out of Work," *Newsweek*, February 20, 1978, 80.

37. "G. I. Wounded," *Time*, March 13, 1978, 96.

38. "The Last Jones," *New York Times*, March 5, 1978, 1, 30–36.

39. "Something About a Soldier," *New York Review of Books* (May 4, 1978), 30–31.

40. "Every Soldier, Coming Home," *Saturday Review* 5 (April 15, 1978), 79.

41. "An Eloquent Farewell to Arms," *Chicago Tribune*, February 19, 1978, 1.

42. *Library Journal* 103 (March 1, 1978), 586.

43. "Versions of Jones," *Nation* 227 (October 28, 1978), 448.

SELECTED BIBLIOGRAPHY

• • •

PRIMARY SOURCES

Papers and Manuscripts

There are three sources of James Jones materials. The Beinecke Library of Yale University has several manuscript versions of novels, including a series of versions and revisions of *Go to the Widow-Maker*. There are also a large number of uncataloged letters and papers, beginning in Jones's childhood and continuing up through the publication of *From Here to Eternity* and after, including some materials up through the first years in Paris.

Also uncataloged, and much more extensive, are the James Jones Archives of the Humanities Research Center of the University of Texas at Austin. Here there is some overlap with materials in the Beinecke Library, for Jones, it seems, often kept more than one copy of things he deemed important. But essentially the Archives at Texas comprise letters, miscellaneous papers of all kinds, manuscripts, and some photographs dating from the early 1950s, following the publication of *From Here to Eternity*, to the end of Jones's life, and, indeed, including papers concerned with the publication of *Whistle* and its critical reception.

In the Rare Book Room of the Firestone Library of Princeton University are the Charles Scribner's Sons Files. These have been cataloged. The files on James Jones include a very large number (not all) of his original letters to editors at Scribner's, together with copies of their replies to him. There are some few photographs and a few letters written to Scribner's by readers of Jones's books. The collection begins with letters written in 1945 and ends with a letter from Burroughs Mitchell to Jones, dated November 23, 1964, in which Scribner's frees Jones to make a new contract with another publisher.

Finally, in preparation of this book, some use was made of the Arnold Gingrich Papers, Esquire Magazine Files, in the Michigan Historical Collections, Bentley Historical Library of the University of Michigan.

Bibliography

John R. Hopkins, *James Jones: A Checklist*. Detroit: Bruccoli Clark/Gale Research Co., 1974.

Works by James Jones

BOOKS

From Here to Eternity. New York: Charles Scribner's Sons, 1951; London: Collins, 1952.

Some Came Running. New York: Charles Scribner's Sons, 1958; London: Collins (Abridged), 1959.

The Pistol. New York: Charles Scribner's Sons, 1959; London: Collins, 1959.

The Thin Red Line. New York: Charles Scribner's Sons, 1962; London: Collins, 1963.

Go to the Widow-Maker. New York: Delacorte Press, 1967; London: Collins, 1967.

The Ice-Cream Headache and Other Stories: The Short Fiction of James Jones. New York: Delacorte Press, 1968; London, Collins, 1968. This collection contains the following short stories: "Temper of Steel," first published *Atlantic Monthly* 181 (March 1948), 32–35; "The Way It Was," first published *Harper's* 198 (June 1949), 90–97; "Greater Love," first published *Colliers* 127 (June 30, 1951), 18–19; "Two Legs for the Two of Us," first published *Esquire* 36 (September 1951); "None Sing So Wildly," first published *New World Writing No. 2*, 7–20, New York: New American Library, 1952; "The King," first published *Playboy* 2 (October 1955), 25, 53–56; "A Bottle of Cream," first published *New World Writing No. 13*, 267–79, New York: New American Library, 1958; "Just Like the Girl," first published *Playboy* 5 (January 1958), 23, 34, 42, 69–70; "The Tennis Game," first published *Esquire* 49 (January 1958), 60–64.

The Merry Month of May. New York: Delacorte Press, 1971; London: Collins, 1971.

A Touch of Danger. New York: Doubleday, 1973; London: Collins, 1973.

Viet Journal. New York: Delacorte Press, 1974.

Whistle: A Work-in-Progress by James Jones (with Foreword by James Jones). Bloomfield Hills, Mich., and Columbia, S.C.: Bruccoli Clark, 1974.

WWII. New York: Grosset & Dunlap, 1975.

Whistle. New York: Delacorte Press, 1978; London: Collins, 1978. An excerpt from this book, "Million-Dollar Wound," appeared in *Esquire* 58 (November 1977), 106–10, 198, 200.

ANTHOLOGY APPEARANCES

"None Sing So Wildly," *New World Writing* no. 2, 7–20. New York: New American Library, 1952.

"Two Legs for the Two of Us," *The Esquire Treasury,* edited by Arnold Gingrich, 220–27. New York: Simon and Schuster, 1953.

"Living in a Trailer," *Ten Years of Holiday,* 202–11. New York: Simon and Schuster, 1956.

"The Thirty-Year Man" (Exerpt from *From Here to Eternity*) in *The Best Short Stories of World War II,* edited by Charles A. Fenton, 47–64. New York: Viking, 1957.

"A Bottle of Cream," *New World Writing* no. 13, 267–79. New York: New American Library, 1958.

"The Valentine," *Ten Modern American Short Stories,* edited by David A. Sohn, 54–66. New York: Bantam, 1965.

Introduction, *The Almost Revolution* by Allan Priaulx and Sanford J. Ungar. New York: Dell, 1969.

MISCELLANEOUS ARTICLES AND PIECES IN JOURNALS

"Buying out of Vietnam: Three Women, Three Prices" (excerpt from *Viet Journal*), *Oui* 2 (November 1973), 39, 40, 116.

"Flippers! Gin! Weight Belt! Gin! Faceplate! Gin!" *Esquire* 59 (June 1963), 124–27, 128.

"Hawaiian Recall" (excerpt from *Viet Journal*), *Harper's* 248 (February 1974), 27–31.

"In the Shadow of Peace" (excerpt from *Viet Journal*), *New York Times Magazine* (June 10, 1973), 15, 17, 46, 48–50, 54, 56, 59.

"James Jones," in *Authors Take Sides on Vietnam: Two questions on the war in Vietnam answered by the authors of several nations,* edited by Cecil Woolf and John Bagguley. London: Peter Owen, 1967, 143–44.

"Letter Home: Sons of Hemingway," *Esquire* 60 (December 1963), 28, 30, 34, 40, 44. (A trip to Pamplona, Spain.)

"Letter Home," *Esquire* 61 (March 1964), 28, 30, 34. (A visit to Alexander Calder's "new studio.")

"Letter Home," *Esquire* 62 (December 1964), 22, 24. (Skiing in Klosters and Jones's injury there.)

Letter to Lee A. Burress, Jr., printed in Burress' article, "James Jones on Folklore and Ballad," *College English* 21 (December 1959), 164–65.

"Living in a Trailer," *Holiday* 12 (July 1952), 74–79, 81, 83, 120.

"Marshall, Illinois," *Ford Times* 49 (March 1957), 53, 57.

"Phony War Films," *The Saturday Evening Post* 236 (March 30, 1963), 64–67.

"Then and Now," *Paris Review* 9 (Winter–Spring 1965) 158–70. (Round table discussion held at American Students' and Artists' Center, Paris, spring 1964, participants being Janet Flanner, Virgil Thompson, Maria Jolas, Man Ray, John Levec, James Jones, William Gardner Smith.)

"Too Much Symbolism," *The Nation* 176 (May 2, 1953), 369.

"Two Writers Talk It Over," *Esquire* 60 (July 1963), 57–59. (Discussion between James Jones and William Styron.)

Untitled article in *Attacks of Taste*, edited by Evelyn B. Byrne and Otto M. Penzler. New York: Gotham Book Mart, 1971, 26–27.

"Why They Invade the Sea," *New York Times Magazine*, March 14, 1965, 47, 49–50, 52, 55.

INTERVIEWS

Nelson W. Aldrich, Jr., "James Jones," in *Writers at Work: The Paris Review Interviews*, 3d ser., edited by Malcolm Cowley, 231–50. New York: Viking Press, 1967. Also available in *Paris Review* 20 (1959).

Barbara A. Bannon, "Story Behind the Book: James Jones and a Touch of Danger," *Publishers Weekly* 203 (May 7, 1973), 38–39.

Maurice Dolbier, "What NBA Means to Some Past Winners." Book review in *New York Herald Tribune*, March 1, 1959, 2, 11.

John Dorschner, "James Jones," *Tropic* magazine [*Miami Herald*], January 5, 1975, 18–22.

Ken Ho, "Ex-Wolf Hound Takes 'Eternity' . . . To Return To Schofield's Quad D," *Tropic Lightning News*, April 6, 1973.

"James Jones: A Talk Before the End." Interview by Willie Morris, recorded and photographed by R. T. Kahn, in *Book Views* 2 (June 1978), 6–7.

David Morris, "James Jones Talks About Whistle," *East Hampton Star*, July 3, 1975, 11–12.

Dannye Romine, "Jones Will Be Remembered from Here to Eternity," *Charlotte Observer*, May 5, 1977, 2G.

Ira Simmons, "James Jones: Coming Home," Louisville *Courier-Journal & Times,* September 15, 1974, E6.

"The Writer Speaks: A Conversation Between James Jones and Leslie Hanscom." Transcription of radio program in *James Jones: A Checklist,* by John R. Hopkins, 5–18. Detroit: Bruccoli Clark/Gale Research Co., 1974.

SECONDARY SOURCES

Books

Aldridge, John W. *The Devil in the Fire: Retrospective Essays on American Literature and Culture 1951–1971.* New York: Harper's Magazine Press, 1972.

Balakian, Nona, and Charles Simmons, eds. *The Creative Present: Notes on Contemporary American Fiction.* New York: Doubleday, 1963.

Berg, A. Scott. *Max Perkins: Editor of Genius.* New York: Dutton (Thomas Congdon Books), 1978.

Bosworth, Patricia. *Montgomery Clift: A Biography.* New York: Harcourt Brace Jovanovich, 1978.

Breit, Harvey. *The Writer Observed.* Cleveland: World Pub. Co., 1956.

Bryfonski, Dedria, ed. *Contemporary Literary Criticism: Excerpts from Criticism of the Works of Today's Novelists, Poets, Playwrights, and Other Creative Writers.* Detroit: Gale Research Co., 1979.

Giles, James R. *James Jones.* Boston: Twayne Publishers, 1981.

Griffith, Samuel B., II. *The Battle for Guadalcanal.* Philadelphia: J. B. Lippincott, 1963.

Halliwell, Leslie. *Halliwell's Film Guide,* 2d ed. New York: Granada, 1979.

Hart, Jeffrey. *When the Going Was Good!: American Life in the Fifties.* New York: Crown Publishers, 1982.

Hassan, Ihab. *Contemporary American Literature 1945–1972: An Introduction.* New York: Frederick Ungar, 1973.

———. *Radical Innocence: Studies in the Contemporary American Novel.* Princeton: Princeton University Press, 1961.

Ernest Hemingway. Selected Letters 1917–1961. Edited by Carlos Baker. New York: Charles Scribner's Sons, 1981.

Hersey, John. *Into the Valley: A Skirmish of the Marines.* New York: Alfred A. Knopf, 1943.

Hoffman, Daniel, ed. *Harvard Guide to Contemporary American Writing.* Cambridge: Harvard University Press, 1979.

Hoyt, Edwin P. *Guadalcanal.* New York: Stein and Day, 1981.

Illinois: Guide & Gazetteer. Chicago: Rand McNally & Co., 1969.

Jones, Peter G. *War and the Novelist: Appraising the American War Novel.* Columbia, Mo.: University of Missouri Press, 1976.

Leggett, John. *Ross and Tom: Two American Tragedies.* New York: Simon and Schuster, 1974.

Mahon, John K., and Romana Danysh. *Infantry: Part I: Regular Army.* Army Lineage Series. Washington, D.C.: Office of the Chief of Military History, United States Army, 1972.

Mailer, Norman. *Advertisements for Myself.* New York: G. P. Putnam's Sons, 1959.

————. *Cannibals and Christians.* New York: The Dial Press, 1966.

Merillat, Herbert Christian. *Guadalcanal Remembered.* New York: Dodd, Mead, 1982.

Miller, John, Jr. *United States Army in World War II: The War in the Pacific: Guadalcanal: The First Offensive.* Washington, D.C.: Department of the Army, 1949.

Mills, Hilary. *Mailer: A Biography.* New York: Empire Books, 1982.

Minnelli, Vincente (with Hector Arce). *I Remember It Well.* New York: Doubleday & Co., Inc., 1974.

Mitchell, Burroughs. *The Education of an Editor.* New York: Doubleday, 1980.

Moore, Harry T., ed., *Contemporary American Novelists.* Carbondale, Ill.: Southern Illinois University Press, 1964.

Morris, Willie. *James Jones: A Friendship.* New York: Doubleday, 1978.

Perkins, Maxwell. *Editor to Author: The Letters of Maxwell E. Perkins.* Edited by John Hall Wheelock. New York: Charles Scribner's Sons, 1950.

Schulberg, Budd. *The Four Seasons of Success.* New York: Doubleday, 1972.

Sheed, Wilfrid. *The Morning After: Selected Essays and Reviews.* New York: Farrar, Straus & Giroux, 1971.

Styron, William. *This Quiet Dust and Other Writings.* New York: Random House, 1982.

Tropic Lightning: (1 Oct 1941–1 Oct 1966) 25th Infantry Division. Doraville, Ga.: Albert Love Enterprises, Inc., 1966.

Vinson, James, ed. *Contemporary Novelists.* New York: St. Martin's Press, 1972.

Essays and Reviews

Adams, Richard P. "A Second Look at *From Here to Eternity*," *College English* **17** (January 1956), 205–10.

Bell, Pearl K. "The Wars of James Jones," *Commentary* **65** (April 1978), 90–92.

Besser, Marianne. "Writer's Concentration Camp," *Writer's Digest* **35** (September 1955), 30–34.

Burress, Lee A., Jr. "James Jones on Folklore and Ballad," *College English* **21** (December 1959), 161–65.

Butcher, Lee. "Me and Mr. Jones," *Writer's Digest* **56** (October 1976), 24–25.

Callendar, Newgate. *The New York Times*, May 13, 1973, 38. (Review of *A Touch of Danger.*)

Cantwell, Robert E. *James Jones: Another Eternity?,*" *Newsweek*, November 23, 1953, 102–4, 106–7.

Davis, L. J. "G.I. Jones: The End of the Epic," *The Washington Post* (March 12, 1978), E1–E2. (Review of *Whistle.*)

Dempsey, David. "By Sex Obsessed," *The New York Times*, January 12, 1958, 5, 32. (Review of *Some Came Running.*)

Didion, Joan. "The Coast: Good-Bye, Gentleman-ranker," *Esquire* 88 (October 1977), 50, 60.

Edwards, Thomas R. "Something About a Soldier," *New York Review of Books* 25 (May 4, 1978), 30–31. (Review of *Whistle.*)

Fiedler, Leslie. "James Jones' Dead-End Young Werther: The Bum as Cultural Hero," *Commentary* 12 (September 1951), 252–53.

Frederick, John T. "Fiction of the Second World War," *College English* 17 (January 1956), 197–204.

"From Eternity to Here," *Newsweek*, January 13, 1958, 89–90.

"From Here to Obscenity," *Life* 30 (April 16, 1951), 40.

Gannett, Lewis. "Guadalcanal: Mindlessly, They Prevailed," *New York Herald Tribune*, September 9, 1962, 1. (Review of *The Thin Red Line.*)

Geismar, Maxwell. " 'Numbly They Did the Necessary,' " *The New York Times*, September 9, 1962, 1, 32. (Review of *The Thin Red Line.*)

Gelsanliter, David. "Remembering James Jones," *Writer's Yearbook* 53 (1982), 74–79, 91.

Goodfriend, Arthur. "The Cognoscenti Abroad—II: James Jones's Paris," *Saturday Review* 52 (February 1, 1969), 36–38.

"The Good Life and Jim Jones," *Life* 42 (February 1957), 83–84.

Greenfeld, Josh. "All the Brave Men," *The New York Times*, April 2, 1967, 5, 50. (Review of *Go to the Widow-Maker.*)

Griffith, Ben, Jr. "Rear Rank Robin Hood: James Jones's Folk Hero," *The Georgia Review* 10 (Spring 1956), 41–46.

Helterman, Jeffrey. "James Jones," *Dictionary of Literary Biography.* Vol. 2, *American Novelists Since World War II*, edited by Jeffrey Helterman and Richard Layman. Detroit: Bruccoli Clark/Gale Research, 1978, 244–52.

Hicks, Granville. "James Jones's 'Some Came Running': A Study in Arrogant Primitivism," *New Leader* 41 (January 27, 1958), 20–22.

———. "The Shorter and Better Jones," *Saturday Review* 42 (January 10, 1959), 12.

Jones, Ernest. "Minority Report," *The Nation* 172 (March 17, 1951), 254–55. (Review of *From Here to Eternity.*)

Jones, Robert F. "Murder in the Wine-Dark Sea," *Washington Post*, May 6, 1973, 4–5. (Review of *A Touch of Danger*.)

Kriegel, Leonard. "From the Infected Zones," *The Nation* 226 (April 8, 1978), 404–6. (Review of *Whistle*.)

Krim, Seymour. "Final Tribute," *New Times* 8 (June 10, 1977), 76.

———. "Versions of Jones," *The Nation* 227 (October 28, 1978), 447–48. (Review of Willie Morris' *James Jones: A Friendship*.)

Lasky, Michael S. "James Jones Has Come Home to Whistle," *Writer's Digest* 56 (October 1976), 22–26, 52.

"Life is a Four-Letter Word," *Time*, January 13, 1958, 96. (Review of *Some Came Running*.)

Macauley, Robie. "Private Jones's Revenge," *Kenyon Review* 13 (Summer 1951), 526–29. (Review of *From Here to Eternity*.)

MacLeish, Kenneth. Île de la Cité, Birthplace of Paris," *National Geographic* 133 (May 1968), 680–719.

Mailer, Norman. "The Big Bite," *Esquire* 59 (June 1963), 23–24, 28, 32.

———. "Some Children of the Goddess," *Esquire* 60 (July 1963), 63–65.

Mewshaw, Michael. "James Jones, Another Side," *The Nation* 226 (April 8, 1978), 406–7.

Moffett, Hugh. "Aging Heavy of the Paris Expatriates," *Life* 63 (August 4, 1967), 30, 32, 34.

Nichols, Lewis. "In and Out of Books," *The New York Times*, January 26, 1958, 8. (Comment on *Some Came Running*.)

Prescott, Peter S. "Warriors Out of Work," *Newsweek*, February 20, 1978, 80, 82. (Review of *Whistle*.)

Pritchard, William H. "Stranger than Truth," *Hudson Review* 24 (Summer 1971), 360–61. (Review of *The Merry Month of May*.)

Ray, David. "A Novel for Teacher," *The Nation* 186 (February 8, 1958), 123–24. (Review of *Some Came Running*.)

———. "Mrs. Handy's Curious Colony," *Chicago* 5 (September 1956), 22–27.

———. "Mrs. Handy's Writing Mill," *London Magazine* 5 (July 1958), 35–41.

Reed, John. "Jones and the Generals," *The New York Times*, March 17, 1974, 4–5. (Review of *Viet Journal*.)

Shaw, Irwin. "James Jones, 1921–1977," *The New York Times*, June 12, 1977, 3, 34.

Sheed, Wilfrid. "The Jones Boy Forever," *Atlantic Monthly* 219 (June 1967), 68–72. (Review of *Go to the Widow-Maker*.)

Smith, William J. "The Innocence and Sincerity of a Regular Guy," *Commonweal* 67 (February 7, 1958), 491. (Review of *Some Came Running*.)

———. "Roughing It," *Commonweal* 69 (February 6, 1959), 500–501. (Review of *The Pistol*.)

Southern, Terry. "Recent Fiction, Part 1: 'When Film Gets Good . . . ,'" *The Nation* 195 (November 17, 1962), 330–32. (Review of *The Thin Red Line.*)

Stevenson, David L. "James Jones and Jack Kerouac: Novelists of Disjunction," in *The Creative Present: Notes on Contemporary American Fiction*, edited by Nona Balakian and Charles Simmons, 195–212. New York: Doubleday, 1963.

Styron, William. "A Friend's Farewell to James Jones," *New York* 10 (June 6, 1977), 40–41.

Sunseri, Alvin. "Quiet Desperation: The Career of James Jones," *The North American Review* 264 (summer 1979), 56–59.

Swados, Harvey. "Through a Glass Sourly Darkly," *The New Republic* 138 (January 27, 1958), 16–17. (Review of *Some Came Running.*)

"Taps for Enlisted Man Jones," *Time*, May 23, 1977, 107. (Obituary notice.)

Thompson, John. "American Gallery," *The New York Times*, April 21, 1968, 52. (Review of *The Ice-Cream Headache and Other Stories.*)

Trippett, Frank. "G.I. Wounded," *Time*, March 13, 1978, 96, 98. (Review of *Whistle.*)

Twentieth Century Authors. First Supplement: *A Bibliographical Dictionary of Modern Literature*, edited by Stanley J. Kunitz and Vineta Colby, 500–501. New York: H. W. Wilson, 1955.

Viorst, Milton. "James Jones and the Phoney Intellectuals," *Esquire* 69 (February 1968), 98–101, 131–32.

Volpe, Edmund L. "James Jones—Norman Mailer," in *Contemporary American Novelists*, edited by Harry T. Moore, 106–19. Carbondale, Ill.: Southen Illinois University Press, 1964.

Whipple, A. B. C. "James Jones and His Angel," *Life* 30 (May 7, 1951), 142, 144, 147, 149, 150, 152, 154, 157.

INDEX

· · ·